OTHER BOOKS BY DAVID FRITH

Runs in the Family (with John Edrich)
'My Dear Victorious Stod'
The Archie Jackson Story
The Fast Men
England v Australia:
  A Pictorial History of the Test Matches Since 1877
Cricket Gallery (ed.)
The Ashes '77 (with Greg Chappell)
Great Moments in Cricket (as 'Andrew Thomas')
The Golden Age of Cricket 1890–1914
The Ashes '79
The Illustrated History of Cricket (ed.)
Thommo (with Jeff Thomson)
Cricket's Golden Summer (with Gerry Wright)
Rothmans Presents 100 Years England v Australia (ed.)
The Slow Men
England v Australia Test Match Records 1877–1985
Pageant of Cricket
Guildford Jubilee 1938–1988
By His Own Hand

STODDY'S MISSION

THE FIRST GREAT TEST SERIES

1894-1895

DAVID FRITH

Queen Anne Press

A QUEEN ANNE PRESS BOOK
First published in Great Britain 1994 by
QUEEN ANNE PRESS
a division of Lennard Associates Limited
Mackerye End
Harpenden
Herts AL5 5DR

A catalogue entry is available from the British Library

ISBN 1 85291 561 7

Set in 10¹/₂/15 Cambridge by Midland Typesetters
Printed in Australia by Southwood Press Pty Limited
Book and cover design by Howard Binns-McDonald

Front cover pictures:
Background, Melbourne Cricket Ground, second Test.
Players,*top left to right,* Richardson, Briggs, MacLaren, Stoddart, Ward.
All pictures in the book are from the author's collection.
10 9 8 7 6 5 4 3 2 1

Contents

Preface _____ vii

1   The Build-Up _____ 1

2   Stoddart's Men _____ 13

3   Southward-Bound _____ 33

4   Australia's Sons _____ 39

5   Those Who Watched and Waited _____ 57

6   Warming Up _____ 65

7   First Test _____ 79

8   A Short Breather _____ 103

9   Second Test _____ 107

10 Third Test _____ 123

11 Upcountry _____ 141

12 Fourth Test _____ 143

13 Drawing Breath _____ 155

14 Fifth Test _____ 159

15 Gliding Home _____ 185

16 What Became of Them _____ 197

Preface

No cricket tour book has been delayed as long as this one, and no Test series has better deserved a chronicle in book form. It comes a century after the event.

Stoddy's Mission is compiled by one who has always been drawn to the period and has gathered a wide variety of source material, a principal element being the 1894-95 England captain's own original tour scrapbook. Out of it came some rich material for his biography—*'My Dear Victorious Stod'* (1970)—in which the 1894-95 tour occupied no more than 35 pages. The bulky scrapbook, together with a mass of detail from other contemporary newspapers, gleaned by my son, Peter, provided a base for the narrative.

Numerous books and periodicals, studied over many years, have bred in the author a familiarity with those long-lost cricketers which has made it sometimes difficult to adjust to the modern game. The happy consequence is that one who is torn in these two directions can at least enjoy the best of both worlds, the old and the new, even if touches of fantasy sometimes intrude. Further complications spring from the fact of having equal backgrounds in and affinities for both England and Australia.

One reference book warrants particular mention for its value in terms of factual framework, and that is Ray Webster's *First-Class Cricket in Australia Volume I 1850-51 to 1941-42*, which affords an 'audited' scorecard of every match, with many longlasting inaccuracies (even from *Wisden*) erased. The skills of Patrick Eagar and Jan Traylen in copying rare photographs are also warmly acknowledged. And, not for the first time, Richard Smart, publisher and friend, is thanked for his crucial support and faith.

Stoddy's Mission comes with the fervent hope that the 1994-95 Ashes Test series between Australia and England—played by way of centenary celebration and watched, courtesy of the new-fangled satellite television, by millions rather than thousands—will be just as breathtaking a spectacle as that First Great Test Series when Anglo-Australian cricket combat took recognisable shape.

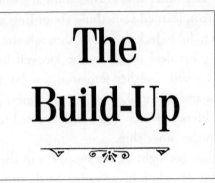

CHAPTER ONE

The Build-Up

The first tour of Australia by an English cricket team had taken place 33 years before, in 1861–62. This was a band of professionals, mostly from Surrey, who were unafraid of seasickness–or, at least, they kept their fear unto themselves as best they could–and keen to pocket the £150 fee together with whatever else they could make by selling bats and other goods that were in short supply in the young colony. The cricketers of New South Wales, Victoria and Tasmania were still far from competent enough to take on the Englishmen on even terms, and all 12 matches with the locals were against teams of 18 or even 22.

Two years after Heathfield Harman Stephenson's 1861–62 pioneering venture, George Parr of Nottinghamshire led the second English team to Australia, having been captain of the very first English overseas tour: to North America in 1859, when the rough Atlantic crossing imposed a reluctance in many of the players ever to risk another sea voyage. Parr, the mighty hitter, triumphantly landed his men in Australia in December 1863 and set about demonstrating English superiority against often feeble opposition in Melbourne, Bendigo and Ballarat–with three weeks in New Zealand halfway through the tour–having come close to losing his life together with the lives of his precious team when their ship was in collision with another vessel soon after setting out from Sydney to Melbourne. The other vessel sank, and Parr, who for a time was frozen with horror, learned something about English phlegm as his best fast bowler, John Jackson, slept through the pandemonium, having sunk a great deal of ale at the farewell lunch in Sydney, while George Tarrant, another ferocious fast bowler (who caught boy Spofforth's imagination), was so overcome by panic that he jumped into a lifeboat which was being lowered to save drowning passengers from the other ship.

Australia at last got sight of the monarch of the game, Dr WG Grace, then aged 25, when he accepted Melbourne Cricket Club's invitation to take out a team in 1873-74. Recently married, WG made this an extended honeymoon, and after a couple of early losses, the Englishmen won consistently, though more easily against the local teams of 15 than 18. Grace had a fair idea of the strength– or more accurately the weakness–of Australian cricket as the two preceding English teams had found it, but by the end of the tour he was prepared to acknowledge that standards were rising. These tours were helping to establish cricket as Australia's national summer game, and the influx of immigrants who played and the settling in Australia of top players Charlie Lawrence and Billy Caffyn, who coached widely and wisely, launched an attitude and a passion which would eventually take Australia to the pinnacle of world cricket.

WG found much to dislike during his long tour: the storms at sea, unruly Australian crowds and bad umpires who were unlikely to improve because of the shortage of first-class cricket, poor-quality pitches ('I take upon myself the credit of having shown the Australians how to prepare a wicket'), and heat, dust and tedious, bumpy journeys in Cobb & Co. coaches.

But he had the companionship of his new wife and young brother Fred, and the comfort of an astronomical tour fee in spite of his amateur status. After going down to an innings defeat by XVIII of Victoria in the opening match, before 40,000 people over the three days, The Champion hit 126 in the next match, at Ballarat, which cheered him up no end. Then came Stawell, where the ground was in 'deplorable condition', one slow delivery plopping into the dust and never reaching the batsman.

Thus Anglo-Australian cricket competition crawled through its early evolution. By now the first Australian team had bravely gone to England. The 1868 combination, led by Charlie Lawrence of Surrey, Ireland, Middlesex and New South Wales, was composed otherwise of Aborigines, full-bloods from Victoria's Western District, Dick-a-Dick, Redcap, Bullocky, Twopenny, the especially gifted Johnny Mullagh and Cuzens, and King Cole, who died in England and was buried in London's Victoria Park and whose remains are now lost forever. It would have been asking too much for European spectators to grasp the true tribal names of these men: Jumgumjen-anuke, Brimbunyah, Bullchanach, and so on. Sri Lanka's Test cricketers of today pose just as great a pronunciation problem, overcome only in reversion to their shorter forenames on their one-day cricket costumes, which are just as garish as those worn by the 1868 Aborigines as they batted and bowled and threw boomerangs and wielded nullanullas and shivered and dreamed of home.

Ten years later, Dave Gregory led the first white Australian team to England. It was a bold—probably even madcap—undertaking, stretching beyond a year from the time the players assembled for the first of a series of matches in Australia and New Zealand, through a gruelling tour of Britain, then, somehow still managing to avoid serious injury or illness among the slim number of only a dozen players, until the final matches in the USA and Canada in the Northern autumn of 1878 and back in Australia. The empty wharf at their departure now rang with cooee calls and thunderous cheers of pride and welcome home.

At last there was a truly Australian cricket team, and from the arduous odyssey heroes had emerged: Charlie Bannerman, the slightly mysterious little batting maestro; Jack Blackham, the courageous wicketkeeper, and Harry Boyle, the artful bowler and 'suicide' fieldsman, Victorians both, with spade beards; and 'Demon' Fred Spofforth, who schemed and terrorised his way to over 750 wickets in this tour of several lands, including his own.

The inspiration behind the tour was John Conway, a visionary Victorian allrounder and journalist, who succeeded in most areas of his awesome scheme, not least in attracting most of the leading cricketers into investing a necessary £150 apiece. This was eventually rewarded with a return of over £1000, an immense sum for that time. And this was in spite of the fact that England had not been prepared to play Australia in an 11-a-side match, a formula which would soon be termed a 'Test match'.

The blue-riband match of the 1878 tour was therefore to be the early encounter with MCC–WG Grace and all–at Lord's. Dave Gregory, with the physique and strut of a blacksmith, led his Australians to victory in one day, stunning London and taking the 'Colonials' a giant step nearer to full acceptance as–at least–equals.

Spofforth was the key agent of irreverence on the day of that cricketing earthquake, May 27: MCC all out for 33 and 19, the Australians 41 and 12 for 1, winners by nine wickets, 4½ playing hours after Frank Allan had sent down the opening delivery to WG. There were 13 MCC ducks in the match, and the match figures for Boyle were 9 for 17, for Spofforth 10 for 20, including a first-innings hat-trick.

> The Australians came down like a wolf on a fold,
> The Marylebone 'cracks' for a trifle were bowled.
> Our Grace before dinner was very soon done,
> And our Grace after dinner did not get a run.

Punch's ironic little ditty underlined the growing suspicion that while cricket was making no noticeable progress in America, Australia might well develop into worthy man-to-man opposition for the full might of England. Some day.

There had already been a match in Australia which was rapidly becoming accepted as the first great even-sided international contest: 'Test match'. It began, at the leafy paddock known as Melbourne Cricket Ground, on March 15, 1877, and ended on the fourth day in victory for Australia by 45 runs. Charlie Bannerman, who faced the first ball, bowled by tubby little Alfred Shaw of Nottingham, scored 165 before retiring hurt with a damaged finger, and Bedfordborn Tom Kendall, slow-medium left-arm bowler, finished England off in the second innings with 7 for 55.

England's team was tough and professional, and yet fell short of what could have been a stronger XI chosen at home from all who would then have been available. But Australia lacked Spofforth, who was the Lillee of his day. He sulked over the omission of wicketkeeper Billy Murdoch, weakening still further Gregory's combination, which already lacked Frank Allan and Edwin Evans. Still Australia won that inaugural Test match. Then, when Spofforth took his place in the side for a second Test 12 days later, and the Englishmen had recovered their poise after a physically demanding and sometimes terrifying spell in New Zealand, James Lillywhite's tourists won by four wickets to spare themselves total disgrace upon their return to the Mother Country.

Things were warming up. Tours were becoming reciprocal. After the 1876–77 tour, the Australians embarked on the aforementioned marathon of 1878, and as they returned to their own shores, Lord Harris's mainly amateur (and distinctly unrepresentative) English team was about to start its Australian tour. They were soon into a match designated as a 'Test', at Melbourne and won for Australia by tiny Alick Bannerman's batting (73) and Spofforth's fierce and clever bowling (6 for 48 and 7 for 62, and Test cricket's first hat-trick). There would have been a second Test on this tour, but a thoroughly nasty match against New South Wales, when ruffians charged onto the field, one of them assaulting Lord Harris, so disgusted His Lordship that he not only cancelled the anticipated big match but saw to it that the next Australian team, which landed in England in 1880, was cold-shouldered by some of the more influential counties. Lord Harris's sense of hurt at Australian betting, drinking and barracking habits was an obstacle to further Anglo-Australian cricket progress.

The breakthrough came when, having been reduced to advertising for matches, and travelling to all sorts of outlying grounds in the North of England and the Midlands, the 1880 Australians were offered a full-scale Test match at The Oval, early in September, the first-ever Test match on English soil. WG Grace led off with 152, which was surpassed by one run by Murdoch when Australia followed on, and England won by five wickets, the captain, none other than Lord Harris (who scored 52), being much gratified, though honest enough to admit that Spofforth's absence through injury had considerable bearing on the outcome.

Enter now the entrepreneurial threesome of Lillywhite (England's first Test captain) and Nottingham professionals and partners Arthur Shrewsbury and Alfred Shaw. They took an all-professional English team, all from the North, to Australia and New Zealand, via America, in 1881–82, and returned home, after initial anxieties, with a tidy profit. And for the first time, four Test matches were played, two each at Melbourne and Sydney. Young 'Joey' Palmer was instrumental in winning Sydney's first Test for Australia by taking 11 wickets with controlled spin variations at a brisk pace, following up with nine wickets, also at the SCG, a fortnight later, when Percy McDonnell pounded 147 against England, the country of his birth. Billy Midwinter, also English-born, and having played for Australia in the first two Tests of all, now represented England, a precursor of the 1993 tug-of-war over British-born and Australian-raised Martin McCague.

While England could always fall back on the claim that a team without WG–and one or two others–could never truly be considered a full England team, Australia could now point to four victories in the eight 'grand' or 'Test' matches now played. And the greatest upset so far was just around the corner.

If society in England was startled by the impudent victory of Gregory's 1878 Australians over MCC at Lord's, it suffered deep shock at Australia's first Test victory in England. In two days in late August 1882, Murdoch's men overthrew a strong England team by force of character. Spofforth took seven wickets in each innings and Hugh Massie's audacious bat brought him 55–easily the highest score of the match–in Australia's second innings. It had rained for two days prior to commencement, and batting was a lottery. England's left-arm bowlers Dick Barlow and Ted Peate hurried Australia out for 63, and England then nosed ahead with 101. Massie's brutal effort took Australia to 122, thus leaving England to make 85 for a fairly routine victory. At 51 for the loss of captain Hornby and Barlow, England were cruising. But Spofforth and his mates were still seething at Grace's running-out of Sammy Jones when the young Australian imprudently left his crease to pat down some divots, and with Ulyett caught behind by Blackham and WG pushing up a catch to mid-off off Boyle, England began to rock. Nerves tightened, and some snapped. Twelve successive four-ball maiden overs went down, and then the collapse continued–to the bitter end. Peate slogged, Boyle hit the stumps, the talented but petrified CT Studd was left not out 0, and the ecstatic Australians were winners by seven runs–probably unaware that one spectator had gnawed right through his umbrella handle and another had dropped dead.

The *Sporting Times* was soon quietly publishing its mock obituary notice for English cricket ... 'the body will be cremated and the ashes taken to Australia' ... a myth which soon became a reality as some women in Melbourne decided to put the ashes of, probably, a bail into a small terracotta urn which was presented, in a handsome velvet bag, to the lofty skipper of the next English team to tour Australia, the Honourable Ivo Bligh. One of the ladies, Florence Morphy, from Beechworth, a music-teacher, married Bligh in 1884, and became a countess in 1900 when her husband succeeded to the title of Earl of Darnley.

Anglo-Australian cricket 'warfare' thus now had a prize over which the two countries would agonise and wrestle ferociously into the 20th Century and beyond, the intensity growing with almost every passing series.

Bligh's 1882–83 team, another short of full strength because of the long period of absence necessitated by sea travel, lost the opening encounter at Melbourne, but Yorkshire's Billy Bates scored 55 and took 14 wickets, including a hat-trick, to usher England to an innings victory on the same ground, and a few days later, at a well-attended Sydney Cricket Ground, England won again, elevating Ivo Bligh, despite his modest personal contributions, to dizzy–temporary–levels of heroism, almost on a par with Nelson and Wellington.

An extra Test was arranged, and Australia spoiled everything by winning it to level the series. But 'St Ivo' had 'recovered the Ashes'. This was the popular, romantic interpretation of events; and though that unpretentious urn remains under lock and key in MCC's museum at Lord's, its symbolism from time to time causes men to take leave of their senses.

Three Test matches were played in England in 1884, the only result going to England, by an innings at Lord's. But the memorable match was the last, at The Oval, when Murdoch, Australia's captain, made the first double-century in Test cricket, and his side, further propelled by centuries from McDonnell and 'Tup' Scott, piled up 551 runs in 9½ hours, Lord Harris giving himself and every other member of his team a bowl, including wicketkeeper Lyttelton, who could not be bothered removing his pads, and took 4 for 19 with underhand lobs. For England, Bill Scotton dragged out 90 runs in almost six hours and Walter Read thrashed a 113-minute century, furious at having been kept back to No. 10 in the order.

Colourful performances were beginning to accumulate, and England v Australia Test cricket was not yet 10 years old.

Four months later they were at it again, in the first five-Test series, staging a Test at Adelaide for the first time. It had the makings of major box-office success too, for England won the first two, only for Australia to come back with the third and fourth Tests, both at Sydney, with all to play for in the fifth Test at Melbourne. But steaming resentment felt by the 1884 Australians at the large tour fees negotiated for the 1884–85 Englishmen (by John Conway, who had arranged the historic 1878 tour) caused the team which played in the first Test to be replaced by the Victorian Cricket Association with a completely new XI for the second. By the end of the series, Australia had had four captains and used 28 players, and the whiff of argument and acrimony had spoiled the summer. Individual performances stood out. Bowlers had scooped up armfuls of wickets, often on wet surfaces, and McDonnell, Billy Barnes, Johnny Briggs, giant George Bonnor, and the 'touch' player from Nottingham, Arthur Shrewsbury, all made hundreds. But the continuity was missing. Even though attendances were high, Australians felt frustration at the sometime absence of star players.

Just over a year later, that frustration was not eased as news filtered in from England of the dismal showing of an under-strength Australian team, led by the hapless HJH Scott. There were squabbles within the ranks, and even Spofforth's presence could not ward off defeat in all three Tests, England winning at Lord's and The Oval by an innings. The batting of Shrewsbury and Grace and the bowling of Barlow, Briggs and Lohmann brought a whitewash that warmed the parlours of England.

They were kept warm that winter too as Shrewsbury's team won both Tests, at Sydney. The first began sensationally, with England humiliated on a responsive turf by newcomers Charlie Turner and Jack Ferris (left-arm), who bowled into each other's footmarks, as they were to do often in the future, dismissing England for 45, still their lowest Test score—if only just—over 100 years later. By the fourth innings, Australia needed 111, a figure which was to take on sinister connotations in the seasons post-Second World War. They managed only 97. The last wicket to fall was that of Spofforth, who left the Test arena forever.

The expression 'Test match' was still anything but universally used. These two 1886–87 matches were, in some quarters, referred to as contests between the 'English Eleven' and 'Combined Eleven of New South Wales and Victoria' or 'Combined Australia' when Jack Lyons and Walter Giffen were enlisted from South Australia for the second match. Here, George Lohmann waded into the Australians with 8 for 35, and just when it seemed he might do it again in the second innings, he received news of his mother's death, and merely went through the motions while Briggs and Bates bowled Australia to another defeat.

Chaos prevailed again a year later, when two English teams sailed to Australia, one led by Lord Hawke, the other by future Hollywood actor C Aubrey Smith. They combined forces for what has since been regarded as the sole Test match of 1887–88, beating a barely representative Australian side by 126 runs after Lohmann (5 for 17) and Bobby Peel (5 for 18) had disposed of Australia, either side of a rainy weekend, for 42. At least one other match during this season of the double tour might have been adopted as a 'Test', but was not. Order scarcely prevailed.

The ocean's sea-lanes were loaded with cricketers again as the two English combinations steamed for home and an Australian side, gathered on a profit-sharing basis again and led by Percy McDonnell, also headed for England for a heavy programme which included three Tests.

Turner and Ferris got through more work proportionately than any pair of bowlers before or since, surely, on that 1888 tour. Medium-pace offbreak bowler Turner took 314 wickets in all matches, Ferris 220. In the three Tests, Turner took 21 wickets, Ferris 11. Their only back-up was Sammy Woods, the Australian-born rugby footballer and boisterous allrounder, now resident in England, and they won the first Test for Australia, on yet another damp and treacherous pitch, at Lord's, with the 40 wickets producing a mere 291 runs. Australia somehow made 61 more of them than did England.

The home side's revenge was crushing: by an innings in two days at a packed Oval, and by a similar margin before lunch on the second day at Old Trafford—all over in 6½ hours. So much for the charm of unprotected pitches.

Two years later the Australians were back in England, led by a returning Murdoch and still finding success elusive, even though the two Test defeats of 1890 were by lesser margins: seven wickets and two. Nothing there to lift the gloom of Australia's struggling economy, even though English cricket was inclined to look back on this time as the start of a 'Golden Age' which lasted until the First World War began at the end of the 1914 summer. It might even have been a source of relief to Murdoch and his sagging squad when the third Test, in Manchester, was washed out completely. Stories of drunkenness and fisticuffs in the Australian ranks had begun to circulate earlier in the tour, *The Bulletin* in Sydney missing no chance to capitalise on the rumours, and it was yet another cricket venture that Australians were somewhat relieved to see laid to rest.

Four years had elapsed since the previous English side had landed in Australia when the greatest figure of all, WG Grace, stepped ashore with his team in November 1891. He was back after 18 years, bigger in girth and in legend, well-paid once again, and with a capable-looking group of players. The heavily wealthy Lord Sheffield was financing the tour (he shrugged off a loss of £2000, and left £150 for the development of cricket in the colony, thus inspiring the creation of the Sheffield Shield). This time Australians were cheered by victories in Melbourne and Sydney which secured the series, the first such success for 10 years, when that celebrated Ashes-creating Test match was won at The Oval in 1882. England gained a consolation win at Adelaide, where Stoddart scored 134 before rain handicapped Australia. The home side were skilfully teased out by Briggs, who took six wickets and repeated himself in the follow-on as Australia sank by an innings. At last, a worthwhile series.

The pause for breath again lasted only a year. Then Jack Blackham and his men took off to England, a promising bunch, though the captain seemed increasingly neurotic and was starting to lose his touch behind the stumps. It was his eighth tour, and any hopes he had of retaining the Ashes were stifled by the runmaking of Shrewsbury, Gunn, Stoddart, FS Jackson and Grace and the pace of Bill Lockwood and Tom Richardson, backed by canny Briggs's slow left-arm. An innings victory at The Oval, with draws either side, at Lord's and Old Trafford, gave England the series, despite Harry Graham's bright beginning with a debut century and Turner and Giffen's persistence with the ball. Once more, Australian papers were left to speculate on all kinds of alleged misbehaviour, mostly off the field but occasionally on it.

England were well pleased, though the total sum of Test cricket in that summer of 1893 was no more than nine days, only the last of them, incredibly, being a Saturday. The Tests attracted big crowds and substantial newspaper coverage, but competed, not always successfully, with 'local derby' county matches and the highly-esteemed Gentlemen v Players games. Middlesex and Yorkshire were two counties which sometimes enjoyed the services of players who had declined Test invitations. International honours were cherished, but in a manner which today could be little understood by sportsmen who psyche themselves up and give every appearance of being prepared to kill for their country. Little survives of Victorian sporting standards.

What cricket now needed at its top level was a Test series on a spectacular scale, to assert the Anglo-Australian bond and to establish once and for all the primacy of Test cricket which was so slow in establishing itself.

The world had little longer to wait.

CHAPTER TWO

Stoddart's Men

A centralised Australian cricket control board was still some way in the future in 1894, but the trend for corporate backing of tours took off when Melbourne Cricket Club and the trustees of Sydney Cricket Ground (still more commonly referred to as 'the Association ground') combined to finance a visit by an English team in 1894–95. The reward was a very substantial profit of £7000, the result not of commercial sponsorship such as logos on players' equipment and shirts or perimeter advertising or broadcasting fees, all of which lay many years in the future. The revenue 100 years ago came from gatemoney, and because the teams were attractive and played some wonderful cricket, ground attendance records were broken throughout Australia. The five Test matches were reported as never before, the narrative compelling, thanks to the long chain of incident and the colourful nature of the players who made it. The *Pall Mall Gazette* broke new ground by publishing—at riskily high expense—long cabled reports from the other side of the world, close on the heels of the action. It was hardly instantaneous, but it kept, in *Wisden*'s words, 'lovers of the game in this country in closer touch with cricket in Australia than they had ever been before'. Even Queen Victoria, not renowned for her interest in cricket, became curious as the public excitement rose, and demanded to be kept up to date on the 1894–95 battle for the Ashes.

AE Stoddart was the chosen English leader. After Lord Sheffield's refusal, 'Stoddy' was the man asked (in February 1894) by the Sydney and Melbourne authorities to raise a good side for the 12th (13th if the twin tours of 1887–88 are both counted) tour of Australia, the ninth to play Test matches. He did his best. There were refusals, of course, and the presence of FS Jackson, Arthur Shrewsbury (Stoddart felt unsure about his health), Billy Gunn, Bobby Abel, Lionel Palairet, HT Hewett, the Rev. William Rashleigh (all batsmen) and 'Dick' Attewell would have strengthened the party considerably. But the combination of 13 players—five amateurs and eight professionals—had all given good accounts of themselves in the 1894 English season and had implicitly pledged loyalty to their captain. As many as nine of them stood an imposing 6ft (183 cm) tall or better, and the average age was 29—a year older than it might have been but for the inclusion of Walter Humphreys, who, at 45, was almost the oldest English cricketer to tour Australia.

ANDREW ERNEST STODDART (Captain) *Amateur*
Born Westoe, County Durham, March 11, 1863
Right-hand batsman, right-arm spin/medium-pace, good fielder
Middlesex 1885–1900 England (16 Tests, 1887–88 to 1897–98)

'Drewy' Stoddart—'Stoddy'—finished the 1894–95 tour as the most popular English captain Australia had yet known, and would have remained warmly in the hearts of Australians just as Arthur Gilligan, Percy Chapman, Gubby Allen and Freddie Brown were to be in Ashes tours that followed, were it not for the disastrous—in several senses—tour which Stoddart undertook three years later. At the conclusion of the 1897–98 tour, his fourth and last, affected by the death of his mother and bruised by defeat and persistent, savage barracking, he spoke out against those who had 'poured insults' upon him and his team throughout the tour. He was suddenly seen in a new light, perhaps as one of the earliest of 'whingeing Poms'.

Stoddart and the kangaroo. England held the Ashes at the
start of the 1894-95 series, but things could have gone
either way as the battle progressed.

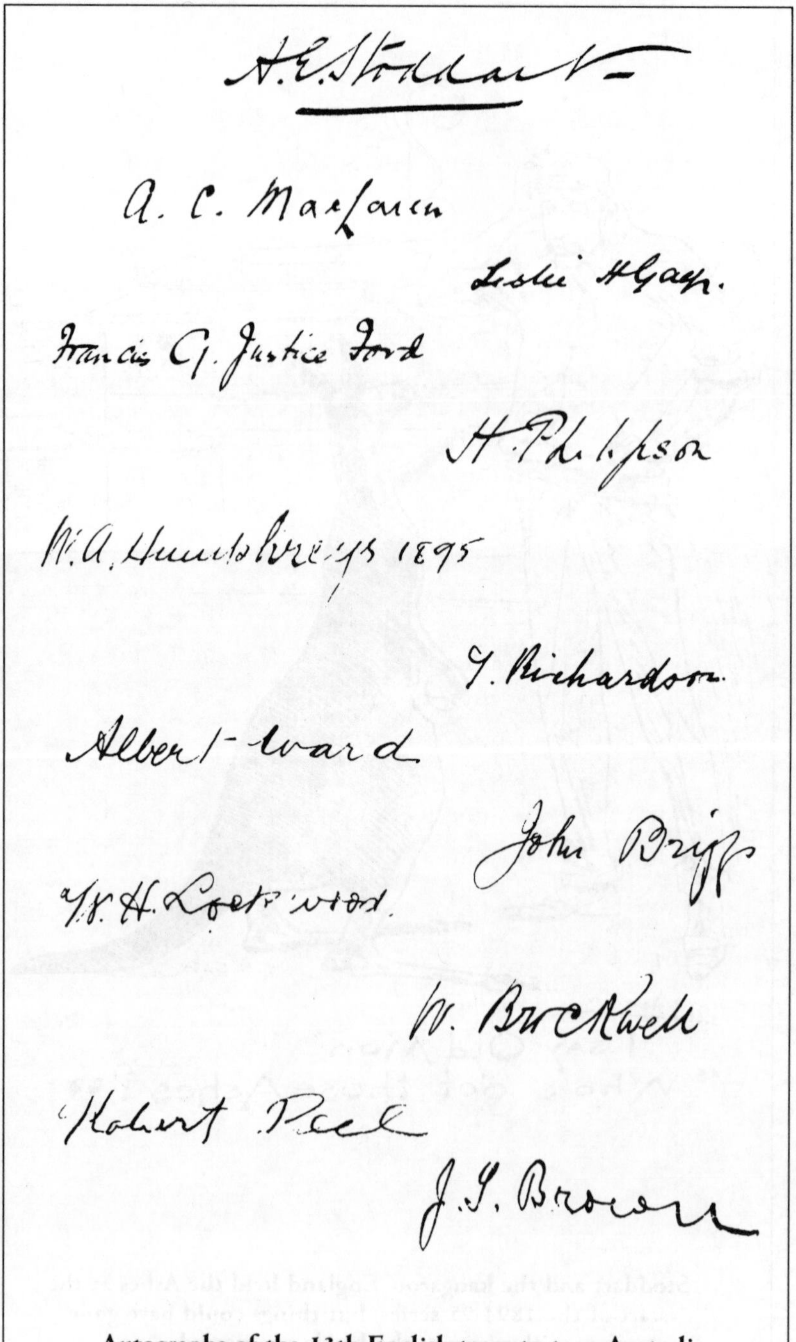

A.E. Stoddart

A. C. MacLaren

Leslie H Gay

Francis G. Justice Ford

H. Philipson

W. A. Humphreys 1895

T. Richardson

Albert Ward

John Briggs

H. H. Lockwood.

W. Brockwell

Robert Peel

J. T. Brown

Autographs of the 13th English team to tour Australia.

'Stoddy'–Andrew Ernest Stoddart–captain of England
at cricket and rugby, and one of the greatest batsmen of the
1890s.

The 1894–95 tour, though, was a glorious passage for him. He had been to Australia in 1887–88, having made the highest score ever recorded to date in 1886, a dashing 485 for Hampstead in a London club match against Stoics, and also established a glowing reputation as an England rugby three-quarter and captain. On his second tour of Australia, in 1891–92, he had scored 134 in 230 minutes in the Adelaide Test, having another of his many big stands with WG Grace (15 years his senior) and looking every bit as polished. By this, his third tour, he was already a favourite. His manner was genial and courteous, which went well with his stature as an elegant champion at two sports.

Born in the North-East, little Drewy moved with his family to London when he was 12. His father was a man of several business interests, including coal-mining, land and wine. The boy was quickly attracted to sport, which was to grip him for the rest of his life. He was capped by England at rugby for the first time in 1884–85, when he was 21, and made his first-class cricket debut for Middlesex a few months later, having made centuries in club cricket with style and almost monotonous regularity. Soon he had become a drawcard at Lord's comparable to Denis Compton a few generations later.

Stoddart played in his first Test match when the two English teams of 1887–88 pooled resources and played Australia at Sydney in the February, a few weeks after he had helped himself to 285 against Eighteen Melbourne Juniors. He seldom threw his wicket away upon reaching 100.

Another fateful event befell him on that first tour. He met a young woman, already married, whom he was eventually to wed almost 20 years later, when he was 43. His name had been linked to many women across the years.

At the end of the 1887–88 Australia tour, Stoddart stayed on to play with the first British rugby touring team and became its leader when RL Seddon drowned while sculling on the Hunter River. The glamorous figure of Stoddart now conquered rugby grounds and even Aussie Rules fixtures—though not all his team-mates could adapt to the alien regime. He pocketed a handsome fee, though this was kept secret at the time. After more football in the 1888–89 English winter, 'Stoddy' got back to cricket again, and in 1890 he actually chose to play for Middlesex against Kent in preference to England against Australia at Lord's, and then again for his county against Yorkshire while the second Test was played. He made himself available for the last Test, at Old Trafford, but it was completely washed out. No question of exhaustion through too many international appearances in those days.

Rugby still had a grip on him, and in 1890–91 he captained the first Barbarians XV. Then, in 1891, he made the highest score of the season, 215 not out against Lancashire at Old Trafford, and was shortly on the ship to Australia, his captain WG Grace.

Stoddart learned from this 1891–92 tour, when Test cricket began to take on a shape that would be recognisable to latterday spectators. He would never lose his sense of joy at hitting the ball not only to the pickets as often as possible but sometimes clean over them, but now a maturity descended over his game. He saw how Abel on one side and Bannerman (Alick) on the other shunned risk and therefore were hardly ever disappointed by dismissal to rash shots. His stature grew with his first Test century in the final match, at Adelaide Oval. When next he was to tread Australian soil, it would be as England's captain.

He was now one of the aristocracy of English batsmanship. He had all the shots, and a natural poise to go with them. When he and Grace batted together, for MCC or the Gentlemen or England, Stoddart often presented the smoother sight. His rugby was drawing to a close, with straps and bandages needed for knees, ankles and an elbow, and a bad game against Scotland to end his international career. But the 1893 Australians were soon taking the field, and 'Stoddy' warmed up with a century in each innings for Middlesex against Nottinghamshire, the first twin hundreds at Lord's since 1817, 76 years before. 'Verily', stated a magazine of the time, 'we are lucky who are living to see such things.'

Stoddart found himself leading England in the Lord's Test, WG having broken a finger. The match was drawn, rain falling on the final (third) day just as Stoddart had made the first-ever declaration in a Test match. He had scored only 24 and 13, falling both times to CTB Turner, who was always a problem for him. But Shrewsbury made 106 and 81, and FS Jackson, whose service to his country in real life prevented him from ever playing in Australia, stroked 91 on debut as England maintained command. Australia's star was the dashing little Victorian, Harry Graham, who chose his maiden Test innings, at Lord's of all venues, to race to his first century in first-class cricket.

In the Oval Test, Stoddart further raised his reputation with an opening stand of 151 with WG Grace, though the younger man had much luck (*The Bulletin* claimed he was dropped 11 times in his 83). This Test was won by England by an innings, and a draw in the third Test ensured that they would go to Australia in a year's time as holders of the Ashes. Stoddart scored 127 for Thornton's XI against the Australians at Scarborough as the summer drew to a close, and then posted his 2000th run, only the third ever to do so, after Grace and Gunn. He was close to being regarded as the world's best batsman at 30.

He was certainly regarded as a man of influence and energy, the qualities needed in any international tour organiser and leader, and when Lord Sheffield declined a second opportunity to take a side to Australia, early in 1894 the men who ran cricket in Melbourne and Sydney issued an invitation to AE Stoddart. Throughout that damp 1894 season he assessed possible recruits for the tour and gradually built up a group of players who seemed to be fit for the exacting experience that awaited them.

So what kind of man was 'Stoddy'? The circumstances surrounding his world-record innings of 485 in 1886 go a long way to explaining: 'The Masher', as he was sometimes known, because of his sartorial elegance, went out dancing the night before, and then sat down for a long session of poker. The young stockbroker found himself winning, so he played on rather than walk away with his friends' money. His play grew wilder as one round of jackpots followed another. He kept winning. Then the signs of dawn light appeared through the windowpane. No point in going to bed now, so they had warm baths and piled into hansom-cabs to the local swimming-pool to freshen up. A hearty breakfast followed, and then he strolled down to the Hampstead ground and was opening the batting at 11.30. Just after 5 o'clock, Stoddart broke the world record of 419 not out and then gave his only chance, a screaming on-drive, which the wretched Stoics fielder muffed. On he went, until at 485 he sent a ball so high into the summer sky that they were on their third run before the catch was safely held. Hampstead finished with 813—no declarations were then permitted—and Stoics did not get a bat.

Was 'Stoddy' now keen to get some sleep? 'Well, perhaps I was, but we had a lawn-tennis match, a four, on that evening, so I had to play that. Then I had another tub, and had to hurry too, because we had a box at the theatre and a supper party afterwards. But after that I got to bed all right, and it wasn't nearly three!'

Three days after his 485, Stoddart hit 207 for Hampstead, and two days after that he was batting for Middlesex in Gloucester and getting out to a WG long-hop for 98. Many a bowler must have hoped, a couple of years later, that there was truth in the rumours that Drewy Stoddart might be about to settle in either America or Australia.

JOHN BRIGGS _____ *Professional*
Born Sutton-in-Ashfield, Notts, October 3, 1862
Slow left-arm bowler, lower-order right-hand batsman, fine cover fielder
Lancashire 1879–1900   England (33 Tests, 1884–85 to 1899)

Bubbly little (5 ft 5 ins) Johnny Briggs was a favourite almost as much in Australia, where he toured six times (this was the fifth), as with his local fans at Old Trafford. He made his first-class debut at the tender age of 16, and it was some time before his often-magical, teasing spin bowling became an even greater asset than his batting and brilliant fielding. He was a talented enough batsman to make 10 centuries, including one against Australia in the New Year Test at Melbourne in 1885. But he was to be remembered best of all for taking over 2000 first-class wickets, including all 10 for 55 against Worcestershire in his final summer of cricket, 1900.

In Tests, he spun out 118 batsmen at just under 18 apiece,

shrewd behind the chuckle, and capitalising on some weak opposition in South Africa in two Tests of questionable status in 1888–89, when he took a record 15 wickets in a day (7 for 17 and 8 for 11) at Newlands, Cape Town.

To Briggs fell the distinction of becoming the first bowler to take 100 Test wickets, when he had Jarvis caught behind in the fourth Test of this 1894–95 series, at Sydney. It would have given this much-loved rolypoly cricketer as much amusement as joy, as when he did the hat-trick in the Sydney Test on the 1891–92 tour.

Among his other triumphs was the Lord's Test of 1886, which he secured for England by an innings by taking 5 for 29 and 6 for 45, with over half his 72 four-ball overs being maidens, such was his accuracy. WG thought that Briggs often tried too much for variation in the course of an over, having the ability to do so much with the ball by way of pace-change, flight and either-way turn.

Though Cardus detected the deeper solemnity of the clown about Briggs, it was his bounciness allied to his skill and the experience of previous tours of Australia which gave Stoddart to believe that in him he had a gem. Besides himself and Briggs, only Philipson (once) and Peel (three times) had previously seen Australia.

WILLIAM BROCKWELL _Professional_
Born Kingston-upon-Thames, Surrey, January 21, 1865
Right-hand batsman and medium-pace bowler, slip fieldsman
Surrey 1886–1903   England (7 Tests, 1893 to 1899)

Billy Brockwell earned himself a trip to Australia by timing his best-ever season to perfection. It came in 1894, when he built upon a promising 1893 season to such an extent that he topped the national averages with 1491 runs at an average of 38.23. His five centuries—in a summer when runmaking overall was at a moderate level—were all made at The Oval, where his popularity skyrocketed.

He seemed to have most of the admirable qualities known to man: 'gentlemanly bearing, geniality and modesty' according to WG. And, with the bat, he liked to play an attacking game, preferably on a pitch of ordinary pace to slow. For years after signing with Surrey he made unspectacular progress, but his experience was being gained in the best of company, for the county was teeming with great names, and won the County Championship eight times (once shared) in the nine seasons from 1887.

In 1893, Brockwell had made over 800 runs and taken 80 wickets, crowning the year with selection by England for the first time, though he did little in the drawn Test against Australia at The Oval, and blotted his reputation by missing Alick Bannerman at slip.

The talent was undoubtedly there, but sometimes a certain wavering of application was suspected. Here was a man who loved travel, the theatre, photography, cycling, and writing—he wrote during this 1894-95 tour for *Sporting Sketches*, the *Windsor Magazine*, *Australian Review of Reviews*, and *Cricket*, with a slightly florid style—and in later years around Surrey a claim circulated that 'Brocky' also loved Tom Richardson's wife. His county and England team-mate's wife, mother of his three children, was to leave Tom around the turn of the century.

Brockwell's charm, coupled with that timely season of supremacy, 1894, had Stoddart writing his name down with eager anticipation.

JOHN THOMAS BROWN_____*Professional*
Born Great Driffield, Yorkshire, August 20, 1869
Right-hand opening batsman, occasional slow bowler, fine fieldsman
Yorkshire 1889-1904 England (8 Tests, 1894-95 to 1899)

The nuggety Yorkshireman Jack Brown was the last man chosen by Stoddart for the tour, following the withdrawal of Abel, and, as it turned out, his selection ultimately had the greatest bearing on the outcome.

A heavy smoker as well as heavy run-scorer, Brown had a developing heart condition to go with his asthma, and trouble with his feet had brought him nearer the wicket, where he now usually fielded most reliably at point. The 1894 summer found him making over 1000 runs for the first of 10 successive seasons, years which were to earn him global accolades for scores of 311 at Bramall Lane, Sheffield and 300 at Chesterfield, the latter being part of a new world-record first-wicket partnership of 554 with John Tunnicliffe. Brockwell and Abel had snatched the previous record from them by one run the previous season.

Brown was the personification of 'Yorkshire grit'. On the short side but powerfully-built, he excelled at the cut and the pull, and somehow seemed at his best when pitch conditions and the match situation were most difficult. He had his own special way of dealing with the short ball on leg stump, and that was to 'half-hit' it—far from artistic but highly effective.

FRANCIS GILBERTSON JUSTICE FORD_____*Amateur*
Born Paddington, London, December 14, 1866
Left-hand batsman and slow bowler, slip fielder
Cambridge University 1887–90, Middlesex 1886–99
England (5 Tests, 1894–95)

Tall and slender Francis Ford foreshadowed two famous names yet to come: Australia's Hunter Hendry for his height and shared nickname of 'Stork', and England's Frank Woolley for his power and elegance as a left-hander who so often conquered fast bowling.

Ford was the youngest of seven cricketing brothers educated at Repton, and a member of a distinguished sporting family. Three of the brothers, including FGJ, were Cambridge Blues, Francis, in his final year, contributing 191 to the University's 703 for 9—then an English record—against Sussex at Hove.

A Middlesex colleague of Stoddart's, 'Alphabet' Ford, as he was also sometimes known, had played in only five Championship matches in the 1894 season, but batted convincingly enough to win a berth on the Australian tour which might not have been his had any of four or five other batsmen been available.

Being an asset in the social setting did Ford's prospects no harm, and his batting potential could well have paid big dividends on Australia's hard pitches. He was, after all, the kind of hitter who could swing a match in an hour, which was the time taken for him to reach a century against the Philadelphians at Lord's in 1897.

LESLIE HEWITT GAY_____*Amateur*
Born Brighton, Sussex, March 24, 1871
Wicketkeeper, right-hand lower-order batsman
Cambridge University 1891–93, Somerset 1894, Hampshire
1900 England (1 Test, 1894–95)

A Hampshire player firstly before that county became first-class, Leslie Gay first found fame at Cambridge, where he represented the University as a wicketkeeper and also as a soccer goalkeeper. His cricket promise was rewarded with selection for the Gentlemen against the Players in 1892, although the Oval match was always seen as less prestigious than the Lord's fixture.

Before long he was being capped by England at soccer, and although he played only four matches for Somerset in 1894, he was selected for Australia by Stoddart, and anticipated becoming a rare double international. The fact that his captain can have had only the briefest sight of him in action–Middlesex v Somerset, Lord's, 1894–suggests that strong recommendation might have come from elsewhere, unless Gay, the 'baby' of the team, struck 'Stoddy' as being good social material, which has always been some sort of factor in English cricket.

WALTER ALEXANDER HUMPHREYS_____*Professional*
Born Southsea, Hampshire, October 28, 1849
Underhand lob bowler, lower-order batsman
Sussex 1871–96, Hampshire 1900

Grey-haired, cheerful and only a month from his 45th birthday when the team sailed for Australia, Walter Humphreys was the biggest gamble of all. He was the last of the underhand bowlers to take big quantities of wickets, but would Australian batsmen, on firm ground and under sweltering sun, become impatient and succumb to this old man's wiles?

A bits-and-pieces player in his early years with Sussex, Humphreys joined the dwindling ranks of the lob bowlers around 1880, and embarrassed three members of the Australian touring side in taking the hat-trick against them for his county. He embarrassed three more four years later when he repeated the feat, the victims this time being McDonnell, Giffen and Scott, top batsmen all. In 1888 he haunted the Australians again with 5 for 21 and 4 for 19 as Sussex pulled off an historic victory, so that Stoddart may not have been anything like alone in believing that the cunning old fox had a mystical hold over the Aussies. 'Even when I had made 200 runs,' said the 1882 Australian captain Billy Murdoch, 'I could not tell from watching his hand which way he meant to turn the ball.'

Humphreys' greatest season was 1893, when he pocketed 122 wickets for Sussex in all county matches at 16 runs apiece, taking eight in an innings three times. One of those occasions involved Middlesex, at Hove, where Stoddart escaped his trickery while making 95 but must have been impressed by the veteran's stamina and repertoire. Nor, as he rode his tricycle around the county, was Humphreys a stranger to the phenomenon of taking all 10 wickets in an innings. For his club, Brighton Brunswick, he did it three times during the 1880s.

WILLIAM HENRY LOCKWOOD _Professional_
Born Old Radford, Notts, March 25, 1868
Right-arm fast bowler, middle-order batsman
Nottinghamshire 1886–87, Surrey 1889–1904   England (12 Tests, 1893 to 1902)

The ranks of the fast bowlers have always reverberated with temperamental members of the fraternity. Bill Lockwood was one of the most volatile. He was as 'on-off' as John Snow of a much later generation, and just as terrifying when his heart was in his work and the rhythm was there. His best year, in numerical terms, was 1892, when he took 151 wickets at a mere 13.60 each, better than either of his two marvellous team-mates, Lohmann and Richardson, the trio bowling Surrey to another Championship.

Surrey—and England—needed his bowling more than his batting, but if he had been solely a batsman he might well have attained international status on that count. Though very seldom batting high in the order, he made 15 centuries in first-class cricket, a lovely drive against the wider off-side ball being the choice shot.

His run-up was not long, and the bounding approach was smooth and easy. Sometimes he was no-balled for touching the return crease, so wide of the line was his usual delivery. Once it left his hand, the ball might hang in the air slightly, enticing a return catch, or, more often, flash in from outside off stump. Murdoch, Fry and Ranjitsinhji were among those who thought Lockwood to be the greatest fast bowler of his time.

With 150 low-cost wickets in 1894, he was a prize asset for Stoddart to have in his Australian expedition, and his place in history was already secure, with Tom Richardson, as the first pair of fast bowlers to win matches by their combined, relentless force.

ARCHIBALD CAMPBELL MACLAREN _____ *Amateur*
Born Manchester, Lancashire, December 1, 1871
Right-hand opening batsman, slip fieldsman
Lancashire 1890–1914   England (35 Tests, 1894–95 to 1909)

Educated at Harrow School, Archie MacLaren was now about to embark on a long Test career which would bring him triumph and controversy in fairly equal measure. A man of independent mind and arrogant manner not only at the batting crease, he came to symbolise the Golden Age of cricket, which corresponded exactly with his period with Lancashire, whom he captained from 1894 to 1907, apart from 1897–98. With his cap-peak almost to the bridge of his nose, moustache bristling, bat held high in readiness, and a dismissiveness both physically and verbally about him, he was a dominant figure.

MacLaren hit a century on his first-class debut when still only 18, and in the season after this first Australian tour of his he batted his way to the world record with 424 against Somerset, a mark which stood for 27 years before Ponsford's 429 for Victoria against Tasmania pushed it into second place.

He had all the strokes and played them with his own personal panache, looking to score off the back foot as much as from his charging drives, with the late-cut a specialty.

If his name is to become immortal he would owe it to fellow Lancastrian Neville Cardus, the patron saint of cricket-writing, who dubbed him the Noblest Roman and never tired of speaking of

MacLaren's 'grandeur', batsmanship which was 'a classical education because of its magnificent outlines'. Most memorably, he liked to describe how Archie 'dismissed the ball from his presence'.

ROBERT PEEL _____ *Professional*
Born Churwell, Leeds, Yorkshire, February 12, 1857
Slow left-arm bowler, lower-order left-hand batsman
Yorkshire 1882–97   England (20 Tests, 1884–85 to 1896)

There may have been some late-Victorian cricket professionals who could match Bobby Peel's hard-playing and hard-drinking propensities, but not many. He was in the unique succession of slow left-arm bowlers produced by Yorkshire—Peate preceded him and Rhodes, Verity and Wardle followed—and took 1775 wickets at 16.20 in a career cut short by his misbehaviour. Over 120 times he took five or more wickets in an innings, with 9 for 22 his best figures, against Somerset at Headingley in 1895. He regularly potted his 100 wickets in a season, and, given the opportunity, made runs, his unbeaten 210 against Warwickshire at Edgbaston in 1896 being described by one enthusiastic pundit as the finest innings yet played by a left-hander.

Peel was to become the first England bowler to take 100 wickets against Australia, and a century later his rate is still second only to Australia's Charlie Turner among the 17 bowlers of both countries in the elite list. Typically for a slow left-armer, he could be lethal on turf saturated by rain—no uncommon thing in days of unprotected pitches. In his very first Test, at Adelaide in 1884–85, Peel had taken some of his eight wickets with the help of a treacherously sodden track, and three years later he and Lohmann, five wickets apiece, bowled Australia out for 42 and 82 on a sticky surface at Sydney. A few months later, back in England, in August 1888, Peel schemed up even better figures with 7 for 31 and 4 for 37, again after some heavy rain, Australia this time losing 18 wickets before lunch on a second day that helped establish Old Trafford as a haven for bowlers more times than not.

Peel was 'like a terrier on a rat' when he identified a batsman's weakness, according to MacLaren. His spin, his trajectory, his speed were all applied according to the needs of pitch and opposing batsman. His cunning was legendary. From his short run-up, Peel, with a bit of a flourish, would hide his bowling arm behind him and then 'fairly whip the ball down'. It could be torture of the slow kind, but just as penetrative as the fire-and-brimstone variety.

HYLTON PHILIPSON_____*Amateur*
Born Tynemouth, Northumberland, June 8, 1866
Wicketkeeper, lower-order right-hand batsman
Oxford University 1887–89, Middlesex 1895–98   England
(5 Tests, 1891–92 to 1894–95)

Born, like Stoddart, in the North-East, Philipson was selected for the 1894–95 tour as first-choice wicketkeeper, having toured Australia three years earlier on the Sheffield/Grace expedition. He was a noted allround sportsman at Eton and Oxford, showing such skill while at the University that he was chosen to play for the Gentlemen against the Players at Lord's and The Oval in 1887. In that season, at Chiswick, he made 150 against Middlesex, putting on 340 with KJ Key and doubtless impressing the toiling Middlesex bowlers, one of whom was AE Stoddart.

'Punch' Philipson went off to India in 1889 with the first-ever English team to tour the subcontinent, and was deputy to Gregor MacGregor on the 1891–92 Australian tour, making his Test debut in the last match, at Adelaide, won by England by an innings. Perhaps Stoddart considered him a lucky player.

It took a very fast bowler to drive him back from behind the stumps. His wicketkeeping style was confident in manner, with a certain gracefulness about it. Lord Hawke described Philipson as 'a lovable personality'.

THOMAS RICHARDSON_____*Professional*
Born Byfleet, Surrey, August 11, 1870
Right-arm fast bowler
Surrey 1892–1904, Somerset 1905   England (14 Tests, 1893 to 1897–98)

'Honest Tom', with his gypsy blood, curly dark hair, and willingness to bowl as fast as he could till he dropped (though he never did drop), was adored by Surrey followers and admired by all opponents. There was a chivalry about him that set him apart, and his strength and great heart placed him on the path to such a phenomenal haul of wickets that for years to come he was regarded by the majority as the best English fast bowler of all.

In only 14 Test matches he took 88 wickets, starting with 10 at Old Trafford in 1893 on his first appearance, and including 54 on his two Australian tours. Over the four seasons 1894 to 1897, Richardson took a staggering total of 1005 wickets, including 290 in 1895. Six times in his career he took 15 wickets in a match, and it did not take his 10 for 45 against Essex in 1894, when he took 196 wickets at the pittance of 10 apiece, to convince Stoddart that he was a certainty for the Australian trip.

He liked the ground to be firm and dry beneath his great boots, and the climax of his run to the wicket came with a leap and a powerful shoulder action, the wrist and fingers applying a lot of off-cut to the ball. His 'breakback' (fast offcutter) was notorious, and got the better of most of his opponents sooner or later. He sought to bowl people out, was accurate, and—in England, at least— seldom dropped short. Nor did he try to be clever with pace-change. He was as honest as his high leading arm.

Earlier in his career, suspicion had been cast on the legitimacy of his bowling action, but if there was a kink in his bowling arm, he soon eliminated it. After he had taken 9 for 47 against Yorkshire at Bramall Lane, with the grinders on the terraces barracking him mercilessly, one of them was asked if they resented his success because of any wrongness in his action. 'We wish the booger did throw,' came the response, 'cos then he wouldn't be the booger that he is!'

ALBERT WARD_____*Professional*
Born Waterloo, Leeds, Yorkshire, November 21, 1865
Right-hand opening batsman, occasional right-arm slow bowler, reliable outfielder

Yorkshire 1886, Lancashire 1889-1904 England (7 Tests, 1893 to 1894-95)

Although no higher than 29th in the national averages in 1894, with 1176 runs at 25.02, Albert Ward was already regarded as one of the soundest batsmen in the land, an ideal component for the touring side to Australia. Tall and calm, patient and determined, he was to average 30.95 in his long career with Lancashire, and it surprised many of his contemporaries that he did not win more than his seven Test caps.

Ward was the prototype opener: no silly risks, settle in, wear 'em down, give the innings a firm spinal column. He liked the cut shot, and played back or forward with a perpendicular bat. Only when he suddenly decided to hit over mid-on did he seem to have a weakness in concentration; but this was a rarity.

On the infrequent occasions when he bowled, he actually sent down a freak ball which years later was identified as a wrong'un, the back-of-the-hand opposite to the legbreak which was developed and given respectability by Bosanquet.

Lord Hawke, monarch of Yorkshire cricket, never forgave the Lancashire scout who lured Ward away, over the Pennines. Although Ward was not under contract to the county of his birth, he was playing for the 2nd XI when the traditional enemy assessed his potential and, in His Lordship's words, 'stole him and bribed him'. The move was profoundly to Lancashire's—and once or twice to England's—benefit.

The Englishmen in their tour uniforms of dark blue with red, white and light-blue stripes. *Standing:* AC MacLaren, FGJ Ford, R Peel, T Richardson, A Ward, LH Gay; *seated:* W Brockwell, AE Stoddart, J Briggs, H Philipson; *in front:* JT Brown, WA Humphreys. The accident-prone Lockwood is missing from the group.

CHAPTER THREE

Southward-
Bound

The 33-week tour began on Friday, September 21, 1894, when the
13 English cricketers, all born in that land, assembled at London's
Fenchurch Street railway station and fought their way through a
colossal throng of cheering, back-slapping admirers. With the
combined Melbourne and Sydney colours—stripes of light blue, red
and white on a dark-blue background—on their neckties and around
their straw boaters, they squeezed through the crowds which
extended from the street, through the booking-hall, up the long
staircase, and along the platform. The reporter from the *Sporting
Life* thought that the loudest cheers were reserved for Stoddart,
Brockwell and Briggs, but they were all given the reception of
established heroes, even though all now was anticipation and
expectation.

The boat-train pulled out at 11.15 am, and at Tilbury a tender
took them to RMS *Ophir*, the largest of the Orient Line fleet at
6910 tons, with a passenger-list of 602. Here, more telegrams
awaited the cricketers, and the tension rose as the hour of goodbye
approached. The wives of Johnny Briggs, Bobby Peel and Walter
Humphreys were there, and Briggs seemed to be fighting a losing
cause in trying to cheer his weeping wife. A few feet away, 'handsome

Farewell to old England. The players line the ship's railing as departure from Tilbury approaches. Nine of them can be identified by their straw boaters.

RMS *Ophir*, 6910 tons, passenger list of 602, the Orient liner which carried Stoddart and his players safely to Australia—and in due course bore most of them home again.

Tom Richardson cast longing eyes after the pretty maiden who left him with more than a suspicion of moisture in her eyes'.

At Fenchurch Street, the last thing the *Star's* man on the spot had seen was 'Andrew Ernest Stoddart's handsome bronzed face beaming out of the train window', but now a slight flush touched that face as the captain responded to a brief champagne toast of farewell, with musical honours, in the ship's smoking-room. He spoke of his team of 'tryers'. The Hon. Ivo Bligh, leader of the famous 1882–83 expedition, whose wife was returning to Melbourne to visit family, joined in the chorus of *For He's A Jolly Good Fellow* as the All Visitors Ashore message echoed round the decks.

Away chugged *Ophir*, under her 10,000 horsepower: first call Plymouth; then Naples on September 30 (where Philipson would join the team); Port Said, October 5; Colombo, October 17; Albany, October 29; Adelaide, November 2.

As the faces lining the ship's rail became indistinct and then invisible, the last vestige of contact for those left standing on the wharf was Bill Lockwood's shrill and faintly desperate whistle.

They were soon into a heavy sea-swell, with mist and rain. In the time it takes modern touring cricketers to zoom from London to Sydney, Stoddart and his men were still tossing in an angry grey ocean, only one-fortieth of the way through their journey. Briggs, Ward and MacLaren alone were well enough to face the first church service, while Stoddart, a good sailor, tried to cheer the rest of his team with personal calls.

Matters improved once *Ophir* had steamed past Gibraltar and into the Mediterranean, though there was a noisy storm as they approached Naples, where Philipson duly came aboard. There was cricket on deck almost daily, and concerts in the evenings. Lockwood went down with a chill. The cricketers gallantly batted left-handed against the team got up from female passengers. And Richardson compensated for his six ducks by taking all 12 wickets for 6.

Into the Indian Ocean they sailed, with the rising temperature the centrepoint of most discussion, and great sunsets for those who strolled the deck. The only serious problem was Peel, who seemed compelled to make mischief. One night he thought it fun to slash his cabin-mate's hammock rope with a carving-knife, sending him thudding to the floor. Next, he locked the same chap in a boiler-room, where the temperature was close to Hell. MacLaren just saved him.

The English cricketers had another big greeting when they landed in Colombo, Ceylon (now Sri Lanka). Landing at six in the morning, they were playing a local XVIII at 10 o'clock, batting all 13 players themselves and mustering 76, reasonable for men who had not yet found their 'land legs' and were trying to put bat to ball on a pitch which was described as 'shifting sand'. Brown and MacLaren were both out first ball, Ward carried his bat through the innings for 24 not out, and a local youngster named Raffel, fastish left-arm, took 9 for 43. By 1 o'clock ('tiffin time') Mr Vanderspar's local team were 23 for the loss of three wickets—to be all out for 58 by 4 o'clock, Briggs 6 for 6, Lockwood 5 for 10. There was just time for Stoddart's team to reach 88 for 8 in their second innings, Raffel adding to his glory with another five wickets, bowling Stoddart for a second time, something on which to dine out for the rest of his days.

Ophir now carried its sporting cargo down the Indian Ocean, berthing at Albany, Western Australia before braving the Bight across to Adelaide. The campaign was about to begin. And the Australian socialite, Maud Power, whom MacLaren had befriended on the voyage, was destined to be his wife.

CHAPTER FOUR

Australia's Sons

As many as 22 players were to represent Australia in the enthralling 1894-95 Test series as it swung back and forth. Eight of them were destined to play in no more than half-a-dozen Test matches in their lifetimes. All, though, played with a passion which would hardly have compared unfavourably with that of today's Australian cricketers, for all the financial dividends that sponsorship has bestowed in the late 20th Century.

JOHN McCARTHY BLACKHAM
Born North Fitzroy, Melbourne, May 11, 1854
Wicketkeeper, lower-order batsman
Victoria 1874-75 to 1894-95   Australia (35 Tests, 1876-77 to 1894-95)

Jack Blackham captained Australia in the first Test of 1894-95, but a damaged thumb and the strain on a 40-year-old in such a gruelling match were to render it his last.

Even in the eyes of most Englishmen, Blackham, in his prime, had been supreme among wicketkeepers. In his flimsy leg-guards and lightly-padded gloves (still to be seen in Melbourne Cricket Club's museum) he stood, usually, up at the stumps even to the fiery Spofforth and even when the bounce was unpredictable.

He was a veteran of the first-ever Test, at Melbourne in 1877, and was easily the last survivor in international playing terms. He was a member of the first eight teams to tour England, and eventually his earnings from cricket enabled him to give up his job at the Colonial Bank. Bank work, though, could never have been as hard on his nerves as cricket. In tense situations he died a thousand deaths.

Throughout his long career he suffered injuries too, mainly to ribs, fingers and teeth. But he was a 'natural' who revolutionised the art of wicketkeeping, helping, alongside several 'new-age' English wicketkeepers, to render the longstop position obsolete, thus giving the bowler an extra fieldsman.

Blackham was highly-respected and friendly, an intelligent crick-eter, who was entrusted with the captaincy of Australia for the 1891–92 series and the 1893 tour of England, having tasted the honour during the agonised 1884–85 series. And his captaincy of Victoria was a major element in that State's resurgence. WG Grace awarded him the palm, and the sensitive Victorian with the trademark spade beard truly earned, through his many years behind the stumps, the accolade 'Prince of Stumpers'.

WILLIAM BRUCE
Born South Yarra, Melbourne, May 22, 1864
Left-hand batsman, left-arm medium-pace bowler
Victoria 1882–83 to 1903–04   Australia (14 Tests, 1884–85 to 1894–95)

Billy Bruce had promised much. At 19 he had made the highest score recorded to date (1883–84) in Australia with an innings of 328 not out for Melbourne against Hotham, and he had top-scored with 45 in the second innings of his maiden Test, at Melbourne in 1884–85, when he was still only 20.

Tall and slim, he was a solicitor by profession, but took leave to tour England twice, on the ill-fated 1886 tour and in 1893, when he made his highest first-class score, 191 against Oxford & Cambridge Universities at Portsmouth, when the Australians gorged themselves on 843 runs. Earlier, when the English and Australian players merged for a Smokers v Non-Smokers match in Melbourne in 1886–87, Bruce scored 131 in an opening stand with England's champion Arthur Shrewsbury which amounted to 196, and an English magazine ventured the opinion that Bruce was now 'the best batsman in Australia'.

It may not have helped his cause that he seldom batted twice running in the same position in the order, or that his bowling was sometimes used and sometimes not. But the quality was there, and when his confidence was high he was a delight to watch—as when he once hit Bobby Peel clean out of Trent Bridge.

SYDNEY THOMAS CALLAWAY
Born Sydney, February 6, 1868
Right-hand batsman, fast-medium bowler
New South Wales 1888–89 to 1895–96, Canterbury, NZ 1900–01 to 1906–07 Australia (3 Tests, 1891–92 to 1894–95)

Attached to Sydney's prominent Carlton club, Syd Callaway was an allrounder who bowled at a nippy medium-fast pace and first attracted attention in the big-time when he performed well against the 1888 Australian team upon its return from England. Firstly he took wickets for NSW, and then, when McDonnell's team went to Brisbane, Callaway, who was visiting at the time, played for the Queensland XVIII and took six wickets in each innings at low cost. Five for 89 for a Combined Victoria & NSW team against the Australians put him in line for higher honours.

Picking up wickets for his club as if playing against children, Callaway won a place in the Australian side for two Tests in 1891–92, without making headlines, but had the satisfaction of getting the wicket of the world's most famous cricketer, WG Grace, in both the Englishmen's matches against NSW.

Callaway toured New Zealand in 1890 and took 51 wickets at only seven runs each, 47 of them bowled, which helped him form an affection for that country that would change the course of his life.

ARTHUR CONINGHAM
Born Emerald Hill, South Melbourne, July 14, 1863
Left-arm fast bowler, left-hand lower-order batsman
New South Wales 1892–93 to 1898–99, Queensland 1893–94 to 1895–96   Australia (1 Test, 1894–95)

Few more fascinating men have played cricket for Australia. If anyone was an allrounder it was Coningham: record-breaking runner, oarsman, rifle marksman, billiards player, footballer, swimmer (he was presented with a medal for saving a drowning child during the 1893 tour of England). He also earned his keep in a variety of ways, including a spell as a barber in Glebe, Sydney. He once suddenly realised that he ought to have been taking the field at the Sydney Cricket Ground, and dashed off leaving a cut-throat razor hanging from a customer's cheek.

He was clearly a man who believed in getting his own way, and he was forced into a form of isolation during the 1893 Australian tour of England, when he was left out of key matches despite good performances on most of his given opportunities. He showed his feelings towards the end by gathering sticks and lighting a fire near the boundary at Blackpool when the temperature dropped during the match late in August.

In December 1895, Coningham hit the first century for Queensland in first-class cricket, 151 in 3½ hours, and typically he had threatened to withdraw from the match until the Sydney authorities came up with £10 to cover his fortnight's loss of earnings. During his time as a bookmaker he was quick to display his status as International Cricketer on his leather bag. Volatility was always to be the first quality associated with 'Conny'.

JOSEPH DARLING
Born Glen Osmond, Adelaide, November 21, 1870
Left-hand batsman
South Australia 1893–94 to 1907–08   Australia (34 Tests, 1894–95 to 1905)

Joe Darling, the schoolboy prodigy, was about to embark on a remarkable Test career. Since his knock of 252 for Prince Alfred

College as a 14-year-old (when his gloveless fingers bled from friction against the twine on the bat-handle) he had been marked out for a higher purpose. Only his farming duties delayed his entrance into international cricket.

Short, rugged and quite without frills, he could defend and he could punish, particularly with the pull-shot to short balls. Beyond this obvious batting quality, leadership skills were also apparent. In his four first-class matches before the arrival of Stoddart's team, Darling had made an unbeaten 63 and an 87. The manner of his making those runs further raised the sense of expectation.

GEORGE GIFFEN
Born Norwood, Adelaide, March 27, 1859
Right-hand middle-order batsman, right-arm medium-pace and offspin bowler
South Australia 1877–78 to 1903–04   Australia (31 Tests, 1881–82 to 1896)

It is spot-on as well as convenient to label George Giffen as 'the WG Grace of Australia'. He dominated most of the encounters in which he took part, either with bat or ball or often both, and his effectiveness was augmented by a dominant personality. He was not as jovial as the English champion, which was a shortcoming for the Australian, midst the tensions of touring and of team-selection, and it is tempting to speculate that Giffen might have been an even greater cricketer had he been endowed with less of a temperamental nature.

Tirelessness was among his qualities. When he was captain, it was said, he acted as if he were the whole eleven. In Giffen's language, a change of bowling was to take himself off only to have a go immediately at the other end. Nonetheless, this was seldom good news for batsmen, for his nagging offspin hardly ever gave scope for liberties.

His greatest performance in statistical terms was an innings of 271 in seven hours backed by bowling figures of 9 for 96 and 7 for 70 in a total of 76 six-ball overs, all in the one match for South Australia against Victoria at Adelaide Oval in November 1891.

George Giffen, Post Office employee and compulsive, tireless
cricketer. He led Australia for the last four Tests of the
1894-95 series.

Even Grace never quite matched that, or Noble or Hirst or Hammond or Sobers. And yet all Giffen had done was improve on his 237 and 12 for 192 in the previous season, against the same opposition, only at Melbourne. Twice before he had taken a century off Victoria and coupled the deed with 13 or 14 wickets. His was a towering presence, prematurely grey, sometimes grumpy, perpetually concerned at the effect his cricket absences were having on his prospects for advancement in the Post Office.

He developed a sound and somewhat dour batting technique, but this and his bowling skill—with subtle pace-changes the potent factor—brought him the 1000 runs/100 wickets double in Tests against England, a distinction he shared with only Noble and Rhodes until Botham came along.

He argued with umpires sometimes, and even with his captains when on tour. He went to England five times and declined a place on the 1888 and 1890 expeditions. He performed the 1000/100 double on the last three tours, testimony not only to his skill but to his fitness. Giffen took all 10 wickets for 66 (like Arthur Mailey of a succeeding generation), for an Australian XI against a Combined XI at Sydney in 1883–84, the first instance in an Australian first-class match, and he did the hat-trick as many as three times, in an unlikely combination of venues: Old Trafford, Adelaide, and Wembley. Not even WG did that.

HENRY GRAHAM
Born Carlton, Melbourne, November 22, 1870
Right-hand middle-order batsman
Victoria 1892–93 to 1902–03, Otago, NZ 1903–04 to 1906–07
Australia (6 Tests, 1893 to 1896)

Harry Graham, the 'Little Dasher', was a day younger than Joe Darling. He made his name with a century in his first Test innings, that innings happening to be at Lord's, in 1893, when Australia were in fearful trouble at 75 for 5 in reply to England's 334. Graham walked in at No. 7, and hit a return catch to Lockwood, who had taken all five wickets. The catch went down.

Graham, 5ft 6ins (168 cm) and under 10 stone, with the even

smaller Syd Gregory, set about mounting a recovery, and though Mold's speed tested them, and Lockwood came back hungry for more, they held steady, running impertinent singles. 'Grummy' Graham's fifty came in only 55 minutes, and the stand raced to 142 in a bare 100 minutes before Gregory was caught behind, Lockwood's sixth victim. More luck had come Graham's way at 57 when Shrewsbury missed him at point off Lockwood, but little more than two hours after he had reached the crease in Australia's dark hour, he found himself on 98. Again, he hit towards point. Shrewsbury stuck up a hand—and the catch fell to ground. Soon the hundred was his, the first by an Australian in a Lord's Test, and made well inside a year since he had first played big cricket. His 107 took 140 minutes, with 12 fours and a five (overthrows), and his immortality—as long as cricket books are read—was assured.

That match was drawn, thanks to Harry Graham's great hand and rain on the last day, but the next Test, at Old Trafford, was lost by an innings, and he made a duck and 42. He finished top of the 1893 tour averages in all matches, piling up 1492 runs at 28.69. But he hardly made a run in the six matches in North America on the way home, and those close to him began to feel concern at his lack of personal discipline. He was by no means exceptional in liking a few drinks.

His electrifying bursts were still worth waiting for, as when he followed his Manchester Test duck with a four-hour 219 against Derbyshire, chanceless and enchanting.

SYDNEY EDWARD GREGORY
Born Moore Park, Sydney, April 14, 1870
Right-hand batsman, excellent cover fieldsman
New South Wales 1889–90 to 1911–12   Australia (58 Tests, 1890 to 1912)

Syd 'Tich' Gregory was some time in finding his feet at Test level, and yet he was to go on to play a record number of times for Australia against England (52) and to notch a great distinction for himself in this 1894–95 series.

He was a member of Australia's first great cricket family. His father, Ned, and uncle, Dave, both played in the first of all Test matches, and he himself was born in the small house provided by the Sydney Cricket Ground trustees in the precincts of the ground itself for his father as curator. Syd's other uncles, Charles and Arthur, played for NSW; his cousin Jack became as great an allrounder as Australian cricket has known; and Harry Donnan (five Tests for Australia) was his brother-in-law.

He lived for cricket, and it showed in his lithe fielding as much as his batting. There was no hesitation for him in the matter of touring either, exhausting and repetitive though it could be. He went on eight tours of England between 1890 and 1912. A popular tourist, he delighted with his footwork, which helped him overcome his conspicuous lack of height, and preferred to play an attacking game, even though he could defend grimly when required. Noting that Gregory was 'rather fond of running himself out', English maestro CB Fry clearly admired him: 'This very great Australian batsman, a little man with beady black eyes and as neat as a domino, had no superior in technique as a cutter and off-driver.'

John Harry
Born Ballarat, Victoria, August 1, 1857
Right-hand batsman, variety bowler, wicketkeeper
Victoria 1883-84 to 1897-98   Australia (1 Test, 1894-95)

Jack Harry was a rarity among 19th Century Australian cricketers in that he made a living from the game and was thus designated as a 'professional'. He was a rarity, too, in that he was sometimes known to tire of bowling with his right arm and switch to left, occasionally achieving his aim of confusing the batsman.

He hit a couple of centuries for Victoria, and collected many runs and wickets for Bendigo and for East Melbourne in club cricket. He was also an interstate baseballer.

Francis Adams Iredale
Born Surry Hills, Sydney, June 19, 1867
Right-hand batsman, outfielder
New South Wales 1888-89 to 1901-02   Australia (14 Tests, 1894-95 to 1899)

After hinting at big things for several seasons, Frank Iredale came through in the mid-1890s as unarguably one of the best batsmen in Australia. He was one of those batsmen who take time to get settled, vulnerable before 20. Thereafter he could be so solid that bowlers developed feelings of futility. The cut was his most prolific stroke, and, unusually for a tall man, he pulled effectively. 'Noss' Iredale was also a sound fieldsman in the deep, the sort whom an opposing batsman who had lofted a shot in his direction scarcely bothered to watch as the catch descended.

ARTHUR HARWOOD JARVIS
Born Hindmarsh, Adelaide, October 19, 1860
Wicketkeeper, lower-order right-hand batsman
South Australia 1877–78 to 1900–01   Australia (11 Tests, 1884–85 to 1894–95)

Blackham's understudy on four tours of England between 1880 and 1893, 'Affie' Jarvis might have earned more Test caps in another era. Instead, his State benefited from his play for over 20 years. He caught the eye when only 18, having a good game against Lord Harris's English team in 1878–79, remaining for years in consideration for higher honours. He had his days as a batsman, notably when he made his highest Test score, 82, at Melbourne in the 1884–85 series, while his five catches and a stumping at Sydney in the next Test helped Australia to a six-run victory. Admiring his attacking batsmanship, his South Australia captain, Giffen, once thought Jarvis was the best batsman in the State. He was also impressed by the fact that, in contrast to the Victorian, Blackham, Jarvis had no unsound fingers on either hand.

ERNEST JONES
Born Auburn, South Australia, September 30, 1869
Fast bowler, good mid-off fieldsman
South Australia 1892–93 to 1902–03, Western Australia 1906–07 to 1907–08   Australia (19 Tests, 1894–95 to 1902–03)

Ernie Jones utilised his Samson-like body for mining, stevedoring and fast bowling. He was Australia's first truly ferocious pace bowler.

Wicketkeepers and longstops, let alone batsmen, found him a terrifying proposition with the new ball, and even after he reduced his storming run-up by a few yards, it was still anyone's guess as to whether he or Tom Richardson was the fastest bowler in the world. Jones was more erratic, and his velocity dropped off slightly earlier than Richardson's. Still, he was, for years, Australia's warhead.

There was a suspicion about the legitimacy of his action—no great rarity at the time—but never any doubt about the danger that always lurked for batsmen when 'Jonah' had the ball. Sometimes he was a threat even when he didn't have it, for when a bouncer broke FS Jackson's rib, Ernie was so sympathetic that when he next met the aristocratic Englishman he warmly shook his hand, almost turning his fingers to splinters with his mighty grip.

JOHN JAMES LYONS
Born Gawler, South Australia, May 21, 1863
Right-hand opening batsman, right-arm medium-pace bowler
South Australia 1884-85 to 1899-1900   Australia (14 Tests, 1886-87 to 1897-98)

Jack Lyons won a place in the game's culture for his shattering attacks on all kinds of bowling—except, perhaps, the slow tempters sometimes floated down by the likes of Peel. At times it seemed that the faster they bowled the harder Lyons hit; and all with a minimum of feet-movement. He was considered more effective than other fabled Australian hitters of the time, such as Bonnor, McDonnell and Massie, because his range extended to the entire compass of the ground. And, of course, nothing pleased him more than to thump the ball clean out of the ground.

On the 1893 tour of England he waded into the MCC bowlers at Lord's to such effect that his hundred came in an hour, and there were 22 fours in his final 149. Alick Bannerman had played doggedly alongside all this time, and when Lyons was caught at long-off, the follow-on arrears of 181 had just been wiped away. It was an innings discussed in cricket circles for many years to follow. On the previous tour, in 1890, he had not done quite so well against MCC: he made 99 in 75 minutes, which paired nicely with his 45-minute 55 in the Lord's Test, which in turn paired well with his 5 for 30 in England's first innings. His 134 in the Sydney Test of 1891–92 came in only 2¾ hours.

THOMAS ROBERT MCKIBBIN
Born Raglan, Bathurst, NSW, December 10, 1870
Right-arm medium-pace/offbreak bowler, left-hand lower-order batsman, slip fielder
New South Wales 1894–95 to 1898–99   Australia (5 Tests, 1894–95 to 1897–98)

Tom McKibbin, a country cricketer, made a quiet debut for NSW against Stoddart's 1894–95 team after his sharply-spun bowling had attracted attention in high places, and soon he was in the Test team, seen by the optimists as another CTB Turner. At times he turned the ball, on responsive pitches, much too far; but when the touch was right, he was a formidable opponent. There were, however, murmurs about his action. They were not factional. There was unquestionably something irregular about his arm movement, quick though it was.

In only his third first-class match McKibbin routed Queensland with 5 for 19 and 9 for 68 at Brisbane, a performance which provided the Test selectors with a temptation they simply could not resist.

CHARLES EDWARD MCLEOD
Born Port Melbourne, October 24, 1869
Right-hand batsman, right-arm medium-pace bowler
Victoria 1893–94 to 1903–04   Australia (17 Tests, 1894–95 to 1905)

Younger brother of Bob McLeod, who played in six Tests in the early 1890s, Charlie, too, was a steady player, more a bowler to start with, before his batting developed. Patience was a keynote, with his bat usually immaculately straight, but in 179 first-class innings his highest score was no greater than 112. Such players, of course, are often valuable to a captain by way of 'ballast', and succeeding Australian skippers continued to find a place for him. And if he should ever have been barracked for slow batting, he had an affliction which, for once, would have been an asset: he was almost totally deaf. Not that this helped him in the 1897 Sydney Test, when he left his crease without realising he had been bowled by a no-ball. The English wicketkeeper whipped out the stumps and, as the law then stood, poor McLeod had to keep on walking to the dressing-room.

HENRY MOSES
Born Windsor, NSW, February 13, 1858
Left-hand batsman
New South Wales 1881–82 to 1894–95   Australia (6 Tests, 1886–87 to 1894–95)

Harry Moses was a polished left-hander who would have toured several times with the Australians but for the containment of his business career. He first played for his country in a Test at Sydney which saw England bowled out for 45 and yet go on to win by 13 runs. Moses was joint top-scorer with 31 in Australia's first innings of 119 and top-scorer with 24 in the disastrous second innings of 97. He top-scored (28) again in the Test which followed, also on his home ground of Sydney, and made second-top-score of 33 in the second innings.

That 33 was to remain his highest score in 10 visits to the crease in Test matches, a cruel reflection of his real ability. At one time he was the highest runmaker in matches between NSW and Victoria, and his 297 not out against the old southern enemy in 1888, at Sydney, was a classic which lasted 10¼ hours. He had warmed up with a century for his State against Shrewsbury's English team. There can be little doubt that had Moses made himself available for one of the many tours of England mounted during his playing days, his reputation in both countries would have been greater. As it is, he was destined, together with so many of his contemporary internationals, to fade into the shadows of time.

JOHN COLE REEDMAN
Born Gilberton, Adelaide, October 9, 1865
Right-hand batsman, right-arm medium-pace bowler

South Australia 1887–88 to 1908–09 Australia (1 Test, 1894–95)

'Dinny' Reedman, a postman, gave long and faithful service to South Australia, and added to his pride with one Test cap. He was a utilitarian batsman, maker of two centuries in his 21 years of top cricket, and a bowler of not quite the first rank, whose day sometimes dawned, as when he took 13 wickets against Victoria when in his 40th year. If there was one aspect of his game which really stood out it was his fielding, throwing and catching. He sometimes captained his State.

ALBERT EDWIN TROTT
Born Abbotsford, Melbourne, February 6, 1873
Right-hand middle-order batsman, right-arm fast/variety bowler
Victoria 1892–93 to 1895–96, Middlesex 1898–1910, Hawke's Bay, NZ 1901–02 Australia (3 Tests, 1894–95), England (2 Tests, 1898–99)

Albert Trott may not have been the most intellectual of cricketers, but he was a willing, powerful batsman and a bowler who could get people out with pace, swing, cut, spin and sheer surprise. Younger brother of Harry, who had already toured England three times, 'Alberto' wanted to succeed at cricket, and practised for long hours, bowling at a large wooden crate in front of a wicket. The crate was Giffen in his mind's eye; the wicket was repeatedly battered by curving balls; the crate, being inanimate, was indifferent to the subtle pace-changes—unlike hundreds of hapless batsmen.

He was playing good club cricket in Melbourne at 15, and at 20 made his debut for Victoria. After only six first-class matches he was chosen to play for Australia, and the deeds he performed from the very first day seemed to suggest the arrival of a great allrounder. Brother Harry was proud ... for the time being.

GEORGE HENRY STEVENS TROTT
Born Collingwood, Melbourne, August 5, 1866
Right-hand batsman, legbreak bowler, point fieldsman

Victoria 1885-86 to 1907-08   Australia (24 Tests, 1888 to 1897-98)

To the start of the 1894-95 series, Harry Trott had only one decent Test score behind him, a defiant 92 in a rearguard action at The Oval in 1893, when England won by an innings. But this Melbourne postman's reputation as a batsman was already soundly established through his deeds in Victoria's matches and on his first three tours of England. His State recognised his captaincy qualities, for his shrewdness shone out in defiance of his sparse education, and his popularity was universal. His manner was equable, and he possessed that uncommon knack of being able to handle players of every sort of personality and disposition.

HUGH TRUMBLE
Born Abbotsford, Melbourne, May 12, 1867
Right-arm offspin bowler, lower-order batsman, slip fielder
Victoria 1887-88 to 1903-04   Australia (32 Tests, 1890 to 1903-04)

A towering bowler of considerable importance to Australia's cause, 'Little Eva' to team-mates, relished by English onlookers as the 'Victorian Cornstalk', Trumble brought the ball down from a rare height, usually with naturally flighted offspin, sometimes with surprising nip off the pitch, and occasionally turning from leg–a sort of Curtly Ambrose at slow-medium pace with 'lateral' movement. He often batted impressively too, and was regarded as one of the better fieldsmen at slip or slightly deeper. Success at international level was slow in coming, though he had developed well on the first two of his eventual five tours of England. Son of an Irish immigrant, brother of John who had already played for Australia, Hugh was a bank employee, and upon joining Melbourne Cricket Club he found himself sharing the attack with the veteran Fred Spofforth– and returning better season's figures. Intelligent, with strong fingers, he absorbed the advice proffered by the likes of Blackham and became a formidable bowler. He also had the dry humour vital to a player who inevitably would sometimes see catches go down midst unrewarded spells of bowling.

CHARLES THOMAS BIASS TURNER
Born Bathurst, NSW, November 16, 1862
Right-arm medium-pace offspin, lower/middle-order batsman
New South Wales 1882–83 to 1909–10   Australia (17 Tests,
1886–87 to 1894–95)

Charlie Turner–'The Terror'–was a fine batsman: the young Ranjitsinhji never forgot a century he saw him make at The Oval in 1888. But his precision bowling, especially when in tandem with left-armer Jack Ferris (they bowled into each other's footmarks) on damp pitches, placed him among the immortals.

Turner's English father was a free immigrant, and the lad used to rise at 4.30 am to work on the Cobb & Co. mail coaches as they passed through Bathurst, and then practise with a mate down at the local oval. Here he developed his extraordinary accuracy, which was coupled with an ability to turn the ball from the off for anything up to a foot, almost always hitting the stumps. He generated lift too, and cultivated a wicket-taking change of pace.

On his first tour of England, in 1888, having taken an abiding record number of wickets (106) in the Australian season, he dismissed 283 batsmen (314 in all matches) at 11.68 a time, Ferris doing almost as well. They were nearly as effective again on the next tour of England, in 1890; and yet both times the Australians' tour record was dismal. About 5ft 9ins tall, Turner had a longish approach to the wicket and an easy action, the arm fairly high, the chest facing the batsman. His yorker was a regular source of destruction, and a number of eminent batsmen of his time gave him the laurel as the best bowler of them all.

The signs were there from the start, for at Sydney, in 1887, his first day in Test cricket found him taking 6 for 15 as England slid to their lowest total ever, 45. And yet Australia lost. Same story next Test, though Turner took 9 for 93 in the match; and again a year later, still at Sydney, when he took 12 for 87, and still Australia lost. Twenty-one wickets at 12.43 in the three Tests in England in 1888 could not prevent a 1–2 deficit for the tourists; and so it went on: Turner, timed at 55 mph, taking wickets galore but often being let down by his batsmen.

He had married at 19, but his wife died soon afterwards. He remarried in 1891, and was ready to add to his 83 Test wickets as Stoddart and his men landed.

John Worrall
Born Maryborough, Victoria, May 12, 1861
Right-hand batsman, roundarm bowler, close fielder
Victoria 1883–84 to 1901–02   Australia (11 Tests, 1884–85 to 1899)

Jack Worrall served Victoria for years as a steady batsman who had begun as an attacker. His first tour of England, in 1888, had been a sobering experience, with a top score of 46 on the mocking succession of wet pitches, and he tightened up eventually to become an opener. His bowling, slowish roundarm, was often useful, and he was one of the game's thinkers. His rugged style reflected his prominence as an Aussie Rules footballer.

CHAPTER FIVE

Those Who Watched and Waited

State Premiers and Governors and politicians; women in the elaborate hats and copious yet cool finery of the late 19th Century, parasols held demurely; tradesmen in their bowler hats, stetsons and straw boaters, with wing collars, waistcoats and watch-chains; homesick immigrants young and old; dreaming office clerks, warm in their jackets; opinionated men from the professions, some in top-hats; seething republicans, moustaches drooping; romantic club cricketers; pilgrims from bush outposts, dust still on their boots; schoolboys in knickerbockers or short pants and straw hats; militia men, splendid in uniform: they all filed through turnstile and members' gate to watch the 1894–95 Test matches.

And many of those who couldn't get to the match joined the overheated scrummages on the pavements outside newspaper offices as the progress of the Tests was posted on scoreboards in the display windows. The cheering was loud and uninhibited, the conversational exchanges high in speculation and, as always in such groups, heavy with borrowed opinion.

The clamour was just as intense at newspaper offices in England as details were rushed into edition after edition. Victoria RI, of course, had no need to join the crush. The Queen evinces the keenest interest,' stated one paper, 'in the Anglo-Australian cricket matches which are now being proceeded with, and has all the telegrams brought to her the moment they are received. It may truly be said that her subjects share her sentiments, for no cricket matches ever played have excited so much enthusiasm.'

At peak times during the Test series business stood still—even at the Ballarat Stock Exchange, where victory and defeat sent a London-born sharebroker soaring off into *Rule Britannia* in 'a tenor voice of high register', soon to be challenged by some Australian brokers who raised the Southern Cross to flap alongside the British flag and lustily sang *The Men of Australia*. Then a Cornishman leapt onto a chair and hollered: 'Look here, you! It's all very well, you talking about Hingland and Hostralia, but where would you all be without Cornwall, eh?' And they all burst into *God Save the Queen*.

Communications between the Melbourne Exchange and Ballarat were limited one afternoon to a wire which read: 'Nothing doing; cricket mad; Stoddart out.'

To be there was everything, for there was no TV substitute, or even action close-ups in the newspapers. A Captain Lee, in command of *Arawatta*, even delayed her sailing from the Port of Melbourne during the second Test match so that he could witness more of the cricket in person. Hunger for news of the Tests even spread to the maritime species. When the mail steamer *Arcadia* berthed at Adelaide, passengers raced to the Oval to watch the stirring third Test, with many of the crew left on board making do with updates as various launches came to and fro. When *Arcadia* sailed, on the Saturday evening, with Australia well placed, she passed sister ship *Himalaya*, out of Melbourne, and flying the signal 'How's the cricket?' The score was flown in reply.

'Felix', the former Australian batsman Tom Horan, often devoted as much space in his columns in *The Australasian* to the people he met at matches as to describing the matches themselves. In writing about the opening day of the final Test, at Melbourne, he noted that one friend had travelled 1300 miles to be there, another 1800. He was told by one acquaintance that 'all the boats from Sydney are packed'. His sympathy went out to all those who had not made it to this historic match; but at least Ned Gregory was there, maker of the first Test duck in the very first Test, 18 years earlier, also at the MCG, when his brother Dave captained Australia. All must have been relieved to get inside the ground and secure a seat, for, as 'Felix' observed, there were 'cabs rushing to the ground in scores, trams loaded, pedestrians making the pace hot so as not to lose the toss'.

During the peak days of the Test series, spectators who failed to get a seat or a good vantage point at least had first access to the food and drink outlets. At Melbourne ('Felix' again), 'the people were literally banked up round the rink, the great trees appearing to grow out of a vast bed of straw hats ... the pavilion enclosure could not have held another man and given him even a glimpse of the wickets'.

As for a land riven by industrial unrest and struggling against economic depression, the man from the *Argus* wrote: 'A wise government desiring to improve our credit abroad might do worse than send away thousands of photographs of the scene on the Melbourne Cricket Ground on Saturday. There appears to be an idea somewhere else that there is a depression here. To the spectator on Saturday that word had no meaning. Stoddart ought to make an excellent agent-general when he returns and looks in at the Royal Exchange and tells some of the haughty financiers of that poorly-informed institution that Australia is most prosperous, that a happier, better-spirited, better-dressed, and better-behaved crowd could not have been seen than he saw at the Melbourne ground ... He should be able to tell the English people, too, that however anxious we might be to increase our exports, we fought hard to prevent "those Ashes" leaving the country; that all classes, free-traders and the other sort of people were determined to "protect" them at all costs.'

'Felix' found that this deciding Test match 'stirred me strangely' with its huge crowd awaiting the outcome of a cricket match which was for 'the championship of the world', played under 'a serene sky of true Australian blue', with a 'delicious breeze' to moderate the temperature. He cast his imagination further: 'Though the old folks

Members of the 'Sydney Push', their society portraits pasted into Drewy Stoddart's tour scrapbook. *Top:* Miss Cox and Mrs A MacArthur; *centre:* Mrs Bowden-Smith; *bottom right:* Miss MacArthur; *bottom left:* the mysterious 'M'.

at home are freezing and snowbound, they are warm to boiling-point in their interest in this wonderful encounter, and I'll wager a trifle that in India and the States the cable messages giving the results of this meeting on the beautiful Melbourne ground are waited for and read with an avidity not second to that which is shown in Adelaide, Sydney, Brisbane, Hobart, Launceston, Dunedin, Christchurch, or any other city, town, or hamlet in Australasia.'

'Queen Bee' was equally smitten by the scene at the MCG during the second Test, two months previously: 'There was a very large muster of ladies in the reserve ... their bright dresses made the scene brilliant'; but she complained of cramped accommodation, many of the female spectators having been forced to stand all day, and there was irritation at the narrowness of the promenade, which made walking difficult. 'Muslins were much worn, both flowered and plain, trimmed with lace or ribbon. Crépons and chiffons were also greatly in favour, and most of the hats were very large, which did away with the necessity of using sunshades and parasols.'

Among the celebrities and socialites seen that day were Mrs Ivo Bligh, a Miss James 'in a smart suit of fawn covert coating, with a pink chiffon blouse', the Earl of Yarmouth, the President of the Legislative Council, Bishop Wandsworth of Salisbury, the Bishop of Melbourne, the South Australian Commissioner of Railways, and scores of ladies, some of whose photographs, clipped from magazines, were later stuck into AE Stoddart's tour scrapbook.

The large hats worn by the women, as ever, prompted complaints from those behind them, whose view was interrupted, and the complaints must have been loudest in the smoking pavilion, which was usually the exclusive preserve of the men. The males may also have been a little jealous of the lunch-baskets brought along by the better-prepared ladies.

Away from the matches, interest extended into the courtroom, where, as one judge (a'Beckett) mentioned during a banquet to Stoddart's team, frequent bulletins on the match's progress were gravely handed up by counsel to the Supreme Court Judges in the guise of legal notes.

The spectators in the 'public' or 'outer' areas were naturally the more vocal. Their shouting seems to have been of an almost completely friendly and humorous kind, such as the cry to MacLaren as he hovered underneath a big hit towards the emerging Hill at Sydney. 'Miss it, Archie,' came the urgent shout, 'and you can kiss my sister!' The gentlemanly amateur would not have been used to being addressed by his christian name. The call, which was also addressed to Patsy Hendren on the same ground a generation later, probably preceded either MacLaren's dropped catch from Reedman's bat in the thrilling closing stages of the first Test or the catch which he completed shortly afterwards to end Ernie Jones's brief innings. It was Hendren, it seems, rather than MacLaren who turned to the spectator and explained that he'd clung to the catch because he had no idea what the sister looked like.

There was much conjecture throughout the tour as to various alleged romantic associations, Stoddart the obvious prime target, several of his players by name or unsubtle innuendo. A female journalist in Sydney linked Tom Richardson to an heiress from Armidale, northern NSW: 'but the difficulty in the way is a nice little wife in England'. Billy Brockwell, wrote the same source, 'has paid marked attention to a fair Jewess whose sister is the wife of a famous Sydney cricketer'. All the professionals in the team apart from Brockwell and Brown, it was remarked, were married men, and Briggs seemed never to tire of talking about his little twin sons.

There was no incriminating correspondence stuck into Stoddart's tour scrapbook, merely a note from Gwen Thomas of 20 Bayswater Road, Sydney, written in neat lettering over half-an-inch (10mm) high: *Dear Mr Stoddart, I am a little English girl, and I want you very much to win this test match. I am so sorry you lost the last match. I am only eight years old, and I sit in the big stand near the Governor's box and watch all the game. I hope you will make your usual big score. Your little wellwisher, Gwen Thomas.*

'Stoddy' almost certainly waved in her direction when he took the field.

England and Australia had deeper feelings for each other than is the case 100 years later, but that is not to say that patriotism never showed its ugly head, provoked or otherwise. One well-meaning moderate wrote to *The Bulletin*: 'One Australian characteristic—perhaps, after all, it's only a general human characteristic—is to take a beating badly and to be over-exultant in victory ... I think we have all been a little too cock-a-hoop over the Adelaide win. Let us comport ourselves with moderation in the presence of so game and modest a sportsman as Stoddart.'

'Felix' meanwhile was hugging himself with delight at the Anglo-Australian bond: 'I wish they could stay with us for ever. They are the most popular team that ever came to Australia, and as for their captain, why the reception he gets whenever he comes out to bat makes me feel proud of my countrymen.'

Not all the English cricketers, or their camp followers, were as highly regarded as Stoddart. Writing in a satirical society column during one of the Sydney Test matches, a female observer flicked some acid ink at certain individuals from the Old Country: 'At the wicket, Stoddart stands at the stumps with quite a Piccadilly manner, and an aroma of heels-together and toes-out broods over the whole team. As for the Cornstalks, they seemed all clothes. One fielder's continuations looked like a divided skirt, whereas the visitors "filled their flannels", as was emphatically remarked on the Members' Stand. But some of the objects who flaunted the English colours on the lawn were scarcely a credit to their townies. All the bandy-legged remittance-men in the province, with paper dickies and frayed hems, seemed to have found enough money in their clothes to purchase a blazing party hat-band and necktie in which to totter up and down the grass-plot looking superciliously at the dem'd Australians, don'tcherknow, through raw-edged eyeglasses. One elderly derelict on our social shores even displayed a tri-color cotton handkerchief—but as he was the most broken-kneed of the lot his violent patriotism was scarcely a kindness to the dear mother country.'

Doubtless great-grandfathers of today's ockers.

There was emphatically nothing of the snob about Stoddart. Another periodical remarked that although he was the recipient of numerous invitations from his influential Sydney friends, he 'invariably preferred the elegant comforts, the unparalleled spaciousness, and the surrounding quietude of the Hotel Australia to all the attractions of private Sydney hospitality.'

In the solitude of his hotel room, Stoddart would have written his letters, one of them in reply to Henry James Ashmore, honorary secretary of the Aboriginal Cricket Club in Shellharbour, on the NSW south coast. Ashmore had written to 'Mr. Sttorade Caption' asking if the English team would play 'a game of cricket for honor on the Sydney ground'. He said it would be 'a curiosity for the Sydney people to see a team of us Aboriginals', and asked how much of the gatemoney they would be permitted to keep. But even the bonus offer of a corroboree in the evening failed to persuade England's captain to fit in such a fascinating match.

Indeed, almost from the start, it was a tour that excited such public interest that gimmicks were unnecessary. The 1894-95 Tests were a major topic of conversation in the street, in the workplace, in the classroom and doubtless even among Clancy and his shearing mates down the Lachlan and down the Cooper. Test matches between England and Australia were being confirmed as the premier events in cricket, a status which was to remain unchallenged until well beyond the Second World War.

CHAPTER SIX

Warming Up

The long and often idyllic voyage behind them, the English cricketers braced themselves for the rounds of civic receptions. George Giffen was among those to greet them when *Ophir* reached Adelaide, as was Major Ben Wardill, the Melbourne Cricket Club secretary, representing the club as one of the tour co-organisers. The players shook themselves down at the South Australian Hotel before a mayoral reception at the Town Hall, when Stoddart made a gracious response to the Mayor's enthusiastic welcoming speech, and Wardill caused laughter by saying that Australia might have had the beating of an English combination of five professionals and eight amateurs, 'but, by Gad, we can never beat eight professionals and five amateurs!' which was the combination Stoddart had been compelled to settle on. The skipper was then asked to introduce his team, which he did, in a loud voice above the cheering, as they stood one by one on the platform. Later, a journalist from a 'pink' paper complained that the mayor had been mean with the champagne rations afterwards.

Net practice at Adelaide Oval drew a crowd, and assessments and forecasts sprouted everywhere. Richardson was fast but straight, with an easy action. (He was to take almost a month to adjust his length to Australian pitches.) Brockwell showed a clean, hard and

The English team photographed in Adelaide's Botanical Gardens. *Standing:* JT Brown, LH Gay, AC MacLaren, H Philipson, W Brockwell, J Briggs; *seated:* T Richardson, FGJ Ford, AE Stoddart, WA Humphreys, A Ward; *in front:* R Peel, WH Lockwood, Major BJ Wardill (secretary, Melbourne Cricket Club).

Below: England batting in the tour opener at Gawler: centurymaker Albert Ward on strike, Francis Ford his partner.

'pretty' drive that scattered onlookers behind the bowlers, but old Humphreys, the lob bowler, looked good only for scheming out any inexperienced batsmen—an accurate forecast. Stoddart opened his broad shoulders and hit Peel and Briggs all over the place, followed by Ford, the tall left-hander 'whose height and build suggest an Australian', who also made a good impression. They all worked up a further sweat with some fielding and wicketkeeping practice, adding to the picture of a team of many talents, as described by Jim Phillips in a newspaper interview. Phillips was an itinerant Australian who had bowled for Victoria and Middlesex and was now accompanying the English side as umpire and general factotum, making some extra money with his pen, an unusual combination.

Of all the early opinions, Major Wardill's on Jack Brown was to have the most amusing repercussions: 'He won't get 10 runs in five months, and had better go home.'

The pipeopener was a two-day match at Gawler, against a local Eighteen, after the Englishmen had had a picnic at Mount Lofty. The playing surface was matting over concrete, the thick coating of dandelions had been mown away, and Albert Ward kicked off with a century, Brown with 56, Brockwell 39, Ford 49, Brockwell being surprised at having to change ends every time he hit a ball over the boundary, with five runs awarded. Briggs then spun 10 of the District team out for 94, Humphreys 5 for 29, and Richardson was thought too dangerous to bowl at all on this hard surface. In the follow-on, Gawler made 22 for the loss of five wickets and were satisfied with a draw, though, as the local paper *The Bunyip* reported, the attendances had not been enough to cover the financial guarantee put up by the locals. It might have been otherwise if Jack Lyons, the strong Gawler-born batsman who already had 10 Test caps, had been able to play. As it was, only 900 watched on the Saturday and 500—plus a few hundred schoolchildren let in free— on the Monday.

The team returned to Adelaide by train, and after three free days, took on South Australia, the Sheffield Shield champions, in the opening first-class fixture. Whether through increasing tension or not, Stoddart declined to be interviewed by the *South Australian*

Register's reporter, who might therefore have been among those who enjoyed seeing the Englishmen vanquished by the State side.

They began well enough, making 477, Brown (115) and Stoddart (66) adding 110 in 70 minutes for the third wicket on a good, fast pitch, and only Peel (0) of the first nine batsmen failing to reach 38. George Giffen was as inexhaustible as ever, sending down 53 six-ball overs to take 5 for 175, to which he was to add 6 for 49 and innings of 64 and 58 not out to show that at 35 he was still far from a spent force, having trained hard all winter.

South Australia replied with 383, and though Humphreys took a wicket with his second lob while many of the huge crowd were still giggling, Giffen and young Joe Darling (117) put their side back into the game, another left-hander, 17-year-old Clem Hill, coming in at No. 10 and making 20. It was a pleasantly warm day, a public holiday to mark the Prince of Wales's birthday, and by the end of it, Ward had played on to the local bronco fast bowler Ernie Jones, and the Englishmen were 110 ahead.

On the fourth day, on a pitch still heartless to bowlers, Stoddart's XI managed to collapse to an ignoble 130. The captain again hit carelessly into the outfield, and Giffen worked his way skilfully through the order. By nightfall, South Australia, needing 225 for a gratifying victory, were already 164 for the loss of Lyons, Walter Giffen and Affie Jarvis. 'Dinny' Reedman, who carried his overnight 76 to 83, won himself a Test place with his fine display, and Darling was in at the end with George Giffen, adding an unbeaten 37 to his first-innings century as a glad augury of what would be 10 years of mainly successful combat against England.

Asked why England had lost this opening contest, Stoddart laughingly replied, 'I don't think I could give you a reason if I tried,' adding weightily a little while later, 'We took risks. Your men took none.'

His continuing courtesy was noted, and even if he was invariably reluctant to submit to interview, it was agreed that his general manner 'contrasts distinctly with the bombastic way in which old WG used to swagger about. Stoddy moves among the crowd most unpretentiously, as if he were walking upon velvet.'

The touring team caught the overnight express to Melbourne and emerged at Spencer Street station next morning eager to restore their pride. And they did, after the usual warm welcome speeches at the Town Hall and at a luncheon at the MCG, where Melbourne Cricket Club president Frank Grey Smith made the key address. Phil Sheridan, who was the principal organiser of the tour, said, with a twinkle in his eye, that he would take over as what in modern parlance would be 'liaison officer' once the team went north of Sydney, 'Major Wardill not being sufficiently acquainted with the manners and customs of the Australian blacks' (Wardill was English-born, emigrating to Australia as a young man).

The English team occupied separate hotels, the amateur 'gentle-men' at Scotts in Collins Street, the professionals at the White Hart in Spring Street, 'in the old obnoxious English tradition'.

Their match with Victoria (for whom Trumble was not playing) was another high-scoring affair, but Archie MacLaren towered from the match, stroking a beautiful 228 to go with his 108 for Lancashire on his first-class debut four years earlier. He was tired and 220 not out by the first evening, having shared a stand of 181 with Stoddart, who was now noticeably more cautious, MacLaren keeping himself going, it transpired, with a few whisky-and-sodas.

Play began at 12.15 pm, with lunch at 1.30 and tea at 4 o'clock and close of play 6 pm. In all that time MacLaren gave only one chance, Blackham the wicketkeeper sparing him, as he also did Peel. England, in their colours 'less showy than those of the last English team' (Lord Sheffield's), had a reassuring 379 on the board for four wickets, and were ready to enjoy the concert staged for them that evening by the Lyric Club at the MCG.

They fell away for 416 next day, young Albert Trott taking 6 for 103 with his mixture of pace and spin, and Victoria struggled to 201 for 7 by the close, a fire in the wooden grandstand adding to the excitement. A cigar-butt caused it, and volunteer firemen put it out with a wild spray of water which half-drowned some of the spectators, 11,000 of whom in total were there that day. Briggs and Peel, the left-armers, took the wickets, and old Humphreys, with five men around the boundary and no slip, managed to snare Frank

Walter Humphreys, the underhand lob bowler, in action against Victoria at the MCG.

Laver. But Jack Harry lodged a claim for a place in the Test team with 70, batting at No. 8, and Victoria got up to 306, 110 behind. So bland was the pitch and so full was Richardson's length still, off his 12-yard run-up, that some of the batsmen here, as at Adelaide, did not even bother to wear batting-gloves.

The third day brought brightening weather, the glare troubling the players. Richardson continued to be troubled, too, by his lack of success, and when he left the field, his spikes were bent and worn from his labours on the hard ground. Victoria would have been better placed had they failed to avert the compulsory follow-on, but Blackham refused to connive by throwing tailend wickets away. By the third evening the English XI were already over 300 ahead, with six wickets remaining.

Appreciated by a little old man in a tall hat who ran onto the field and shook his hand, Stoddart added a careful, responsible 78 to his first-innings 77, while Peel (65) and Briggs (43) showed they could bat too, helping their side secure a long lead: 398. By the end of the fourth day, Victoria were 160 for 6; and Peel and Briggs spun them out next day for 253, Harry Trott (63) and Bob McLeod (62) leading the runmaking. The Englishmen, having banked an important win, headed happily off to Sydney.

Over 600 people waited to greet them at Central Station, from where they were driven in drays to the Town Hall. There the Mayor delivered an interesting speech, saying he loved cricket and that Australians were related to 'that great country, England, which possessed to an extraordinary degree the genius of colonisation'. He felt it was remarkable that such a young community could compete on equal terms with the cricketers of the country from which it had sprung. Major Ben Wardill again managed to say the right thing, following Stoddart's elegant response; he felt that these matches helped generate the spirit of Australian federation; and so far the attendances and the takings were up on the previous tour by Grace's team.

The players were then driven to their hotels, the amateurs to the Hotel Australia, the pros to the Empire, and in the evening they were guests at the Lyceum Theatre.

After the run glut of the Victoria match (1353 runs), the New South Wales match threw up fewer runs but much absorbing cricket. The Sydney public must have sensed it, for a record 10,029 turned up on the opening day (paying £479). Lockwood was fit to play, and generated enough pace to have three slips in at the start and to bowl four men out as well as finding the edge frequently. There is record of the Englishmen shouting 'Catch it!' as the ball flew from the bat, proving that it is more than a modern childishness.

Bobby Peel shared the new ball, and between them he and Lockwood did most of the damage as NSW were bowled out for 293, Frank Iredale shoring up the innings with 133. Again there was enormous curiosity about Walter Humphreys, never before seen at Sydney, but the rotund, grey-haired underhand bowler was ineffective again.

As many as 23,579 people crammed in for the second day's play, Saturday, lifting the ground record and again dwarfing the figures for the Lord Sheffield/WG Grace tour of 1891–92. When any umbrella was raised against the sun the owner was instantly shouted at by those whose view it threatened to block, the penalty for resistance being a hail of missiles. So many women were among the gathering that some had to be accommodated in the members' pavilion.

They all saw NSW finish their innings, but by the end the English XI were only 85 behind and only three wickets down. MacLaren, the double-century hero at Melbourne, fell for 4 to Charlie Turner, but Stoddart, 77 and 78 at Melbourne, now made 79, and Jack Brown, having scored a century on his Australian debut at Adelaide, now made another at Sydney, completed on the third day, when the temperature was 98°F in the shade. Brockwell's careful 81 helped the Englishmen to a lead of 101, and when NSW went in again, only the stunted figure of Syd Gregory stayed at the crease for any length of time. He made 87 nice runs in two hours, but Iredale added a duck to his century, and Harry Donnan's 39 was second-highest score. Stoddart's men needed 80 for victory.

In the making of them, for the loss of two wickets, there were two curious incidents to match one similar at Melbourne, when

Harry Graham was the fielder. The fashion of the time seems to
have been that successful catchers tossed the ball in the air; not out
of sight, into the sky, as is the modern practice, but just a few feet
or so. But there was around this time an embarrassing outbreak of
dropped rebounds and consequently disallowed catches.

The NSW supporters were not discouraged, for most of their
men had done something worthwhile. Gregory's innings was thought
to be the best so far played against the Englishmen, and three other
players who were to play Test cricket had made successful debuts:
Tom McKibbin, Bill Howell (5 for 44 in the first innings), and Jim
Kelly, the wicketkeeper who stood up at the stumps to all but the
very fastest bowling, and who bore a fair resemblance to Rod Marsh,
who would fill his place some generations later.

Stoddart's approach was now obvious. Eschewing risks, and deaf
to the barrackers who wanted him to hit out, he was taking his
leadership responsibilities seriously. Callaway had tested him with
some fast stuff at his ribs, which he had played down calmly. Turner,
his old adversary, tempted him in vain (he finished with 1 for 100
in the first innings), but his drives went along the turf, over the
beautifully manicured SCG outfield.

Now he marshalled his players onto the northern mail-train,
bound for Armidale, where XXII of New England tensely awaited
their glamorous overseas visitors.

The Englishmen nearly went north one short. On the Sunday
of the NSW match they had cruised on Sydney Harbour, pulling
into an inlet after lunch. Bill Lockwood bullishly ignored warnings
about sharks and dived in for a swim, while Stoddart and Ford
took potshots with firearms at flotsam in the water. Halfway to the
shore, Lockwood began to struggle and splash and gurgle. Some of
the players reckoned it to be a brilliant impression of a drowning
man. But the Surrey and England fast bowler was genuinely in
trouble, and had a lifebuoy not been thrown to him from a passing
yacht and two of the sailors not brought him round with the aid
of some brandy, England would probably have gone north minus
a key player. It must have taken Stoddart's mind back to 1888,
when he stayed on after his first cricket tour of Australia to play

for the rugby side brought out by Arthur Shrewsbury. The captain, Dick Seddon, had drowned while sculling on the Hunter River, and 'Stoddy' had taken over the leadership.

When the train reached Armidale, Stoddart asked for it to be shunted into a siding so that his men could get a little extra sleep before braving the town's reception. They checked into Tattersall's Hotel at 11 am and began the match at noon before 1400 spectators, whose relief after all the preparations for this great match was undisguised when yesterday's thunderstorms failed either to swamp the ground or to come back next day.

The Englishmen drew lots for the batting order and managed to fade away for 67, to which New England replied with 147, the crafty Humphreys lobbing out 10 of the 22 batsmen for 52 and Richardson perhaps frightening one or two in taking 9 for 46, including a hat-trick. Ford top-scored with 49, MacLaren 44, as the Englishmen made 196 on the second day, avoiding humiliation, and the game was drawn. The chief distraction while they were in northern NSW was a visit to Bakers Creek goldmine, the richest in the State, and then they entrained again, bound for southern Queensland.

Another concrete pitch awaited them at Toowoomba—and, of course, another earnest reception with speeches. All was gaiety, with the newly enlarged grandstand (capacity 260) the central pride. Now it was Leslie Gay's turn to top the score. He made 49 in the English total of 216 in reply to the Toowoomba Eighteen's 113 (Brockwell 8 for 60, Humphreys 9 for 48), and when the Toowoomba second innings closed, Jennings had made himself a local hero by hitting Peel over the boundary not only to save the innings defeat but to leave England insufficient time to make the three runs needed for victory when the 17th and final wicket fell. With typical Queensland generosity, the local captain offered Stoddart time to make those runs, but he refused firmly, thanking him for the thought.

The train journey to Brisbane was not a long one, and there the customary enthusiastic crowd awaited them, QCA officials in their midst. At the reception, Drewy Stoddart began with the curious remark that 'although he had the misfortune to have been born an

Down the mine: another eyeopening experience for the touring cricketers. Brockwell is seated to the left, with Richardson standing behind him; Lockwood stands at the rear, in straw boater, with Ward in front of him, Briggs (arms folded) to the right, Brown (hat-brim turned up) in front of him; Humphreys seated extreme right, with Wardill behind him.

Englishman, he was very proud of his country'. Although more at home with a cricket bat or rugby ball in his hands than making speeches, he was carrying out his duties well, with great charm and diplomacy, though it had been remarked upon in Sydney that 'he can talk well but his natural gentleness makes him swallow the soft mellifluous voice instead of throwing it off his chest'.

This time, having spoken for a couple of minutes, he handed over to his friend Hylton Philipson, one of the two English wicket-keepers, to propose the Mayor's health.

At the Exhibition Ground, where Queensland's first Test match would be played 34 years later (with Don Bradman on debut), only around 500 were present to see the Queensland XI take on Stoddart's English team under a grey sky. A brass band brightened up proceedings, and so did the English captain, as the crowd built up rapidly.

Stoddart's innings, delayed by a 10-minute rain shower, saw him glad to leave another round of speeches behind in the luncheon room, and soon he was into his stride, playing a range of glorious strokes against Coningham, the fast-medium bowler who had had such a disappointing time in England with the 1893 Australians, and Pierce, a skilful lob bowler, and three other striving but unsuccessful bowlers as Percy McDonnell, captain of the 1888 Australians in England, rang the changes. On his way to his century, Stoddart took particular liking to a series of Coningham deliveries, hitting them for 4, 4, 5, 4 and then 6 clean out of the ground. 'Conny' always had a short fuse, and this treatment was stored for future reference. In another match on another day, he would show 'Stoddy' what he thought of him and his fancy batting.

Albert Ward, although the ideal supporting player, batted with charm and style, and the stand of 249 was achieved in only 160 minutes, the Lancastrian finishing with 107, his captain 149 (having been beaten when 98 by a ball which clipped the wicket but failed to disturb the bails)—described as the best innings ever seen in Queensland. MacLaren chimed in with 74 not out and Philipson, at No. 10, took his chance against the wilting bowling by making 59.

Arthur Coningham, undaunted by the efforts of 51 overs (5 for 152), then opened the Queensland innings and scored 43, the highest return in their 121, and on the third day 4000 people turned up to see the last eight wickets go down for 70 to give the English XI an innings victory. Tom Richardson had taken 8 for 52 and 3 for 11, 10 of those 11 wickets bowled, the other lbw.

The team enjoyed its success in the backwaters of Queensland, with a Sunday cruise on SS *Otter* thrown in on the Sunday and success at the races after the match with a £27 dividend on Memory, winner of the one-mile December Handicap. It all helped reduce the tension before the first Test match as they embarked on the long train trip down to Sydney.

CHAPTER SEVEN

First Test

'This was probably the most sensational match ever played either in Australia or in England' pronounced *Wisden*, while giving it merely 19 lines of coverage. The claim still holds true almost to the same degree 100 years later.

The sky over the Sydney Cricket Ground 100 years ago was very much wider. To stand anywhere in the crowd or even out in the centre now is to be surrounded by huge edifices named after Noble, Bradman, O'Reilly and footballer Clive Churchill. Few could have imagined, in December 1894, how the charming and unpretentious little stands and enclosures would one day be swept away in favour of this circle of giant engineering wonders; and fewer still would have had cause to imagine.

All that survives is the gem of a pavilion, with its 'showboat' style, clocktower, minarets and coat of arms, built in 1886, but with the upper decks of the wing structures still a few years in the future.

Moving clockwise, there was a small wooden building serving as the ground secretary's office, and then an awning offering spectators shade. Here the Northern Stand was soon to be erected, to be superseded in time by the MA Noble Stand.

Further to the right, the Paddington Hill was substantial enough

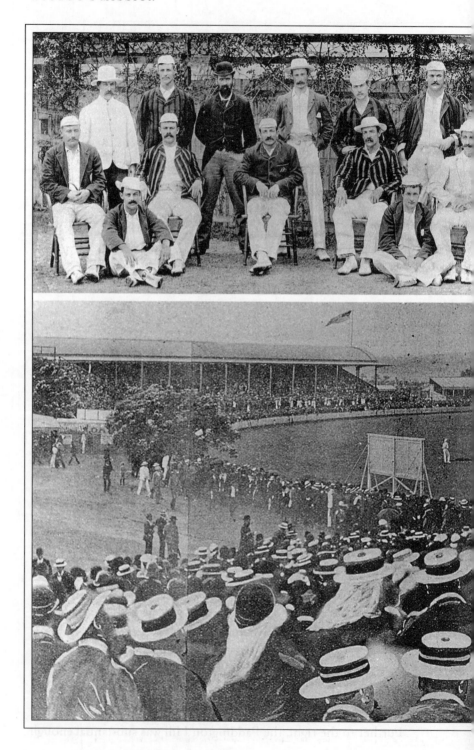

Australia's team for the first Test. *Standing:* C Bannerman (umpire), JC Reedman, JM Blackham (captain), CE McLeod, CTB Turner, JJ Lyons; *seated:* GHS Trott, J Darling, G Giffen, E Jones, FA Iredale; *in front:* SE Gregory, H Graham (12th man).

Sydney Cricket Ground during the opening Test match of the First Great Test Series, when a total attendance of over 60,000 was recorded for the match.

to hold at least a couple of thousand people, and those who had come from the environs of Paddington now had no need to traipse all the way around the perimeter fence to get in. There was now a new entrance off Moore Park Road.

The 'Bob' Stand, parallel with the pitch and stretching down the eastern side of the ground, was to be erected some months later, but viewers in that area at least had a wide canvas awning above them to make life tolerable on the hot days. At the end of it was the scoreboard, viewable from quite a distance, but to be much improved upon by Ned Gregory's progressive construction shortly afterwards.

Then came the Hill, which was merely a wide embankment in 1894, grassy and welcoming, soon to be increased in depth. But the southern end of the ground fell away merely to an open space of natural surface, by way of entrance, with some tents and refreshment booths, where ales could be bought, and lunches for one-and-sixpence (15¢), and even patent medicines. There was not yet a Sheridan Stand, and the cycle track around the boundary would not be laid down for another year or so. But the old Brewongle Stand ran the length of the western side, with its small towers to be added later. It was then known simply as the Grandstand, Brewongle being the trade-name of the tearooms within, and when it was eventually demolished in 1977, some old bottles were dug from the foundations, predating even this 1894–95 Ashes series.

The only other structure, apart from the pavilion, to survive into the 1990s from last century is the Ladies' Stand, but even this was only an architect's sketch in 1894. In that position stood a pretty little pavilion with long side awning painted in stripes.

This was the circumference that the Australian and English cricketers of 1894–95 knew, with the pitch made from Merri Creek soil, soon to be superseded by Bulli soil after the Merri soil had so misbehaved after rain. The pitch was rolled by true horsepower, the animal equipped with special protective leather shoes for its hooves. And surmounting all were the colourful flags, a red one bearing 'SCG' now fluttering from the pavilion for the first time to assert that this was no longer the semi-anonymous 'Association

Cricket Ground' but the *Sydney* Cricket Ground.

FIRST DAY

Jack Blackham spun the coin after Stoddart had remarked that 'Someone will be swearing directly, Jack. I hope it's you!' Blackham, though, won the toss, and word slowly circulated around the crowd of 11,000.

He had only just been confirmed as Australia's captain, having been in a huddle with Giffen and Turner, fellow selectors, in the pavilion to decide the issue. They left Harry Graham out of the XI, and Stoddart omitted Philipson and Humphreys from his tour party of 13. The sun shone brightly, with a few puffy white clouds sailing by, and the umpires, Charlie Bannerman and Jim Phillips, were on their way to the middle, followed by the Englishmen and Australian openers Jack Lyons (one of five South Australians) and Harry Trott. Richardson strode out his run-up, and Peel prepared to take the other end, bowling with the Hill behind him. Play started at 12.12 pm.

All the early doubts about Tom Richardson were now swept aside as the black-haired heavyweight thundered in and bowled Lyons off his pad 10 minutes into the match, the ball running on down to the boundary. Soon, Trott was out almost identically, the off stump being uprooted and broken. Next ball, the first of Joe Darling's long and distinguished Test career, Richardson adjusted his line for the left-hander and burst a yorker through him, the ball taking with it the middle and off stumps. Three down for 21 through sheer force of effort on a blameless pitch.

Giffen and the tall Iredale steadied the innings, though a better pick-up by Briggs at cover point and better glovework by Gay as the throw came in would have seen the end of Iredale early in his innings. Richardson was getting the ball to lift off not too short a length, and Giffen felt he detected a ridge in the pitch. Whether it existed or not, the oldstager held on, taking occasional fours and leaving Stoddart to explore other bowlers: Briggs for Peel, Lockwood for Richardson as lunch loomed. Australia made it safely to the interval at 78 for 3, but only just, for Lockwood had jumped a ball at Giffen's bat-handle and Gay, the keeper, to that infernal cry 'Catch it!', could not hold the chance high to his left.

The strong, reliable Richardson bowled again after lunch, but Giffen was comfortable, and even straight-drove Briggs into the crowd for a five. The accident-prone Lockwood ricked his shoulder in fielding a hard-hit ball and now had to leave the field, Turner substituting for the opposition until Philipson could run on. The match was moving Australia's way as Brockwell and Stoddart himself took punishment from Giffen and Iredale, and it took another change, this time Francis Ford, the tall left-armer, to bring an end to this fourth-wicket stand when it was worth 171. Iredale (81) lifted him to mid-off and Stoddart parried the high ball and pouched the catch, ending a 2½-hour partnership.

Enter, after the tea stoppage, the boylike figure of Syd Gregory— 'Tich'—a special favourite at this ground where he had actually been born, in the groundsman's cottage at the back of the pavilion, his father, Ned, being the SCG curator. Young Syd, when in his early teens, had fallen badly from the moving two-ton roller and was bedridden for months. But he was tough and came from a great and proud cricket dynasty, and he was playing for his country at 20, at Lord's of all places. The trouble was that so far, in 11 Test innings, he had reached double figures only once (57 at Lord's in 1893), having batted everywhere between No. 4 and No. 11 in the order. Here he was again at No. 6; his fielding in the covers was unsurpassed; but when would he get some runs to substantiate his high reputation?

Giffen hit Richardson to the leg boundary to bring up his only Test hundred, having escaped at 90 when Gay juggled and dropped a catch off the same bowler; and now Gregory felt he was seeing the ball well enough, and the pair put 53 runs on the board in one half-hour period, mainly at the expense of the two left-armers, Briggs and Peel, before it was decided that they should play carefully for stumps.

At 5.50 pm, with 10 minutes remaining, Brockwell broke through for England, finding the edge, Ford, who had dropped Gregory on 50, holding the catch. Giffen had batted for 4½ hours for his 161,

England about to take the field at Sydney. MacLaren is talking to a man in dark suit; Stoddart is to the left of MacLaren; Richardson has his hand to his chest; Lockwood is extreme right.

Syd Gregory, Australia's little double-century hero of the first Test, at the Sydney ground where he was born.

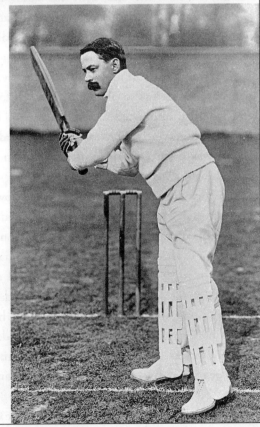

his defence demoralising and his driving controlled and profitable. He stroked 22 fours and a five.

Reedman stayed with Gregory to the close, when the little chap was 85 and the total 346 for 5. Lockwood's absence had hindered England, but had Gay not suffered such an unfortunate day behind the stumps, the tourists might yet have been in control. The wicketkeeper, who had kept goal for England's soccer team, must have felt as if he'd let in six against Scotland. There was little left of his confidence.

SECOND DAY

The buzzing attendance of the opening day was more than doubled, to 24,000, on the Saturday. They were 'all well dressed, well conducted, with the one topic absorbing the attention of all, and the one wish dominant—a good match, and a win for Australia'. Their team's recovery from yesterday's shocking start had radiated feelings of well-being.

Lockwood was still unable to take the field, and his Surrey team-mate Brockwell was soon cursing himself for missing a catch at slip as Richardson bounced one at Reedman. The batsman soon took another lifter, one report said on the head, another on the heart. Either way it stirred him to lift a ball from Peel over the fence and into the animated audience.

Gregory was now 99, and pegged down. Finally, he got his favourite cut shot to the ball, which sped away for two, and his thousands of admirers roared, and went on roaring.

His next three partners, though, soon went: Reedman, in the next over, nicked a slow teaser from Peel to Ford at slip; Charlie McLeod made 15 before Richardson raced in and yorked him; and Turner hung around for a quarter of an hour for a single before touching Peel through to a greatly relieved wicketkeeper. Australia were now 409 for 8, and England's opening batsmen would have been gearing themselves for what seemed an imminent task. Theirs was to be a long wait.

Blackham, the 40-year-old skipper, in his 35th and, as it transpired, final Test match, chose this day to make the highest score of his

Test career, 74 in 86 minutes. In that time he and Gregory hurtled along at two runs a minute, setting an Australian ninth-wicket record of 154 which was still unbeaten 100 years later. Gregory sped to 150, and Blackham raised the 500 by Australia for the first time in a home Test. The Englishmen were exasperated, particularly when the wretched Gay put another catch down, Gregory at 131, off the labouring Peel.

But if Peel was labouring, how much more sweat was Richardson expending? The fast bowler was into his 56th over of the innings before the last wicket was to fall, taking 5 for 181, he and Brockwell taking on the overs which the injured Lockwood might have bowled.

There was great applause for little Gregory when he passed Giffen's 161, and the only hope England felt concerned Blackham's condition. So hectic was the runmaking that the veteran had to call for a drink, which he sipped through his puffing.

Next came Charlie Bannerman's 165 in the first of all Tests. In surpassing that, Gregory became the highest scorer in a Test in Australia. They ran the cheekiest of singles, and Richardson seemed to be going at the knees as he bowled on and on, his pace much reduced.

Gregory got to 194 and then lofted Briggs out towards the long-off fence. Ward ran towards the ball, got a hand to it, dropped it, and it went to the fence. Next ball, Gregory had his double-century, square-cutting Ford for three after four hours at the crease. The reception given him by 'his' crowd was thunderous, and went on for almost five minutes, straw hats curving through the air, parasols jigging up and down, handkerchiefs waving, vocal chords straining. Might the delightful midget now go on and get a triple-century? After all, these Tests were being played without time limit.

Stoddart brought himself back on, and without further ado Gregory slammed him deep on the leg side, where the reliable Yorkshire hands of Peel secured the catch. SE Gregory 201, with 28 fours; Australia 563 for 9, a new Test innings record. Jones was rough on Stoddart before Blackham's extraordinary knock ended, Richardson finding the energy to cut a sizable breakback into his stumps at speed: 586 all out.

Original scorebook sheet from Australia's huge first innings at Sydney, showing Giffen's hundred and Gregory's double-century.

Gregory's admirers were busy in those last minutes: he was soon the glad recipient of a collection of just over £100, which included £25 from the ground trustees, £5 from Melbourne Cricket Club, and £20 from Mr Toohey the brewer. George Houston Reid, the corpulent NSW Premier and future Prime Minister of Australia, handed over the princely sum, leaving the young batsman to gasp 'Thank you' and no more. He had just whispered, white-faced, to a friend: 'What'll I say? I can't make a speech.' He didn't need to. It was enough that he could place the English bowling to all sections of the pickets, no stroke more pleasing than his angelic latecut.

The only steadying note midst the Gregory euphoria was the reminder that Australia had been sent reeling to 3 for 21 by Richardson on the first day before Giffen and Iredale played their superb hands. Also, Blackham's support made Gregory's 201 feasible. And yet the presentation was to Gregory alone. Well, he was the only Sydney man of the four batting heroes; and Australia was still a loose bundle of separate colonies. 'He got the cash,' wrote one critic, 'they had to be content with praise.' But little Syd was such an agreeable fellow that he almost certainly saw to it that his teammates were not empty-handed.

So at last England got to the wicket, and the long exertions in the field showed in MacLaren's early lapse in concentration—caught at cover from a poor stroke off Turner—and Stoddart's tired tread as he took his place.

Jones, the Merv Hughes of his day, steamed in as if to prove he could do anything Richardson could do. But the Englishmen held him at bay, Albert Ward calm and correct, looking for his best shot, the cut, but taking no undue chances. The runs began to flow—until Giffen came on, applying an immediate choke. His stranglehold in the South Australia match was still fresh in English minds, and it may have caused Stoddart's downfall as he played with unusual hesitancy at Giffen and edged into Jones's coarse miner's hands at slip: 43 for 2.

Blackham introduced Harry Trott's legbreaks as Brown tried to settle in. He had been bothered by them in the Victoria match;

but now he fiddled and fudged and eventually hit Trott to the fence, and Turner was reintroduced.

A run-out spoiled it for England. With 35 added, a mix-up as Lyons misfielded and recovered saw the end of Brown, and it needed some sensible play by Brockwell to escort the always watchful Ward through to the close of play, with the gloom encompassing the ground, rain about to fall after long threatening, and England, 130 for 3, very much in second place. It had been a day which would long be associated with Syd Gregory's masterpiece. It was also the day on which news reached Sydney of the death, on December 3, way across the Pacific, in Samoa, of the tubercular Robert Louis Stevenson, whose spirit perhaps imbued this Sydney Test match with a Jekyll-and-Hyde quality.

THIRD DAY

Rain fell on that pitch on Sunday and again before resumption on the Monday, when the crowd was back to 11,000, still a good company. The surface was soft but not dangerous, and the greasy ball made the bowlers' task difficult. Still, Ward, 67 at the start, seemed to believe he should hit out rather than hang around for the impossible delivery, and he fell to a catch at long-on with only eight more runs to his name. This compensated Turner, who had seen a chest-high catch from Brockwell put down by McLeod at cover before the luncheon break.

The sun had dried the ball and firmed the pitch to a dangerous stickiness after the interval, and Harry Trott's legbreaks seemed the biggest problem for England. After Iredale's cool catch in the deep to get Ward out, Peel benefited from yet another catching error in this strange match, this time by Jones at slip, though it mattered little, Gregory, who could do no wrong, catching the left-hander over his shoulder running at mid-off: 155 for 5.

Still over 400 runs in arrears, England found some relief in a Brockwell-Ford stand which saw the pitch ease slightly as 56 were added, Ford batting in his best Lord's manner, Brockwell holding himself in check, taking two hours over his 49. Ford went first, stumped not exactly elegantly by Blackham, who then caught

Brockwell, standing well back to Jones's thunderbolts, the fast bowler's first Test wicket: 211 for 7. The compulsory follow-on loomed as a certainty.

One end of the pitch was appreciably more cut-up than the other, and it may have been Blackham's kindness or simple good fortune for England that Jones was not bowling into the rougher end. As it was, conditions seemed to be easing as Briggs made much more impact with bat than ball, scoring a priceless 57 in two hours. Lockwood at last came into the match with a handy 18, and it was while he and Briggs were resisting that a quick delivery from part-time bowler Lyons split Blackham's thumb, a serious enough injury to have tangible repercussions later in this epic match.

Gay was glad of a return on his generosity to the Australians when England were in the field. Now he himself was reprieved at slip, and with Briggs increasing in confidence with every over, their ninth-wicket stand amounted to 73, the best of the entire innings. Local pundits were now complaining about the absence of Trumble from this match, and left-arm fast man Coningham. They would not have let England off in these conditions.

Giffen got Briggs in the end, with one which kept low, and Gay (33) was caught at cover by Gregory without further addition. England were bowled out for 325, 261 behind, and were obliged to follow on, though there was no time left that evening to start their second innings.

FOURTH DAY

One of Stoddart's concerns now was the growth of grass that slowed the SCG outfield and probably livened up the pitch. But at least the weather was cloudy rather than fiercely sunny, and the pitch was thus quiet. Sawdust was still in evidence at the end of the bowlers' run-ups, and the sight of Turner and Jones with the new ball could have been daunting to England's openers, MacLaren and Ward, with their side 261 in arrears. Nonetheless, MacLaren, always looking for a moneymaking opportunity, plunged £4 on his team at this point at 50–1.

Blackham, his thumb badly cut and the bone damaged, would

Albert Ward of
Lancashire, whose
top score in both
innings had such
a crucial bearing
on England's fate
in the first Test.

The horse-drawn
roller at the
Sydney Cricket
Ground. The
noble beast was
equipped with
special leather
moccasins to
protect the pitch.
Only the rain
presented danger.

never keep wicket for Australia again. McLeod took over.

The Lancashire pair played warily, and only two boundary hits came in the first hour as Giffen and Turner probed. MacLaren was deceived and bowled by Giffen at 26, and Ward should have gone when he was 28, McLeod behind the stumps snatching at a thin edge off Giffen. It was one of history's most expensive misses, and only the most philosophical were reflecting that Blackham's absence merely offset England's loss of Lockwood through most of Australia's innings of 586.

Stoddart batted as cautiously as he had ever done, partly through the needs of the side and partly by way of example to those who would follow. He knew there was no need to influence Ward, who was as sound and solid as Manchester Town Hall.

They eased the Australian stranglehold after lunch, Stoddart once even tapping Giffen to the fence twice in an over. But with 36 to his name, the captain hit Turner to cover and Giffen took a low catch: 115 for 3.

This reunited Ward with Brown, and the total grew—after Brown had overcome his early suspicions about the pitch. By tea England's score had risen to 183, and Ward was 98.

Australia could not do without McLeod's bowling any longer, so Reedman took over as wicketkeeper after tea. Ward's century came with a leg boundary off the eternal Giffen, in only 197 minutes, and was well received, for he was regarded as an amiable and modest man. Half-an-hour later, when he and Brown had added 102, Ward was bowled by a beauty from Giffen as he played back, just as the grey sky gave way to a burst of sunlight. England were now 44 behind overall.

Brockwell, the star of the 1894 English batting season, now played another useful innings, though he soon lost Brown, caught by Jones, arms outstretched at mid-on, for 53. Brockwell and Peel steered England through to close of play, passing the sinister 261 figure which brought them at long last into credit, every run worth two from now on. In this match of fielding disasters, the Australians and their supporters could barely believe it when Jones spilt a simple catch off the leading edge of Peel's bat towards the end. It was, of course, only apparent after the match just how crucial every run and every catch would turn out to be.

FIFTH DAY

Wednesday brought an air of slight disarray, what with McLeod back behind the stumps for Australia, and Turner late, necessitating a second substitute in the field, none other than Briggs, who had yet to bat. Over in Britain, a delay in the cable service meant that the last three days' cricket would eventually all come through at once, causing readers to read the story over and over again in disbelief.

Australia struck an important blow when Jones, on a fuller length, broke through Brockwell with 22 added. Six runs later, Peel stunned a ball from Giffen only to see it dribble back and unseat the bails: 296 for 6, England 35 ahead.

Briggs joined Ford, and it was here that England finally seemed to have a chance of making some sort of match of it, for they put on 89. They ought to have been separated almost at once, for McLeod muffed a stumping chance against Ford off Giffen, whose heart must have been aching, and substitute Graham wobbled about under a skyer from Briggs, off Trott, and grounded the catch. Ford hit Jones hard when he pitched short, and Australian frowns deepened as the same batsman stabbed his bat at the ball when Turner almost had him playing onto his stumps. Dame Fortune now seemed to speak with an English accent.

It was 344 for 6 at lunch, and afterwards Ford launched into Trott and landed the ball over the fence in the direction of the tennis courts. Briggs broke with protocol by taking two boundaries off a Giffen over, and England seemed to have taken command when McLeod, given another spell with his medium-pacers, took a soft return catch from Ford when the Middlesex left-hander was two short of his half-century and then bowled Briggs for a priceless 42.

Tailend runs are always the hardest to countenance by the fielding side, and the Australians now had to wait while Lockwood, a good batsman, and Gay mustered a further 22, and Richardson, the flu-sickened No. 11, made a dozen highly significant runs. With Trott's legspin accounting for Lockwood and Gay, England were out at last in the 182nd over, nine overs more than Australia's mammoth first innings. Their total of 437 meant that the home side needed 177 for victory. That was less than a third of their first-innings score. And the pitch, thanks to the rain, was holding up and not powdering dangerously. Giffen's 75 overs made it 118 for the match, still a record for Australia against England.

With two hours to bat, Lyons started as if he intended to get the 177 singlehanded that evening. In 15 minutes he crashed his way to 25 out of 26. And then Richardson bowled him as he aimed a wild swing. Giffen, showing no great tiredness from his bowling stint of 75 overs (4 for 164), came in at No. 3 and made the greatest contrast to Lyons, pushing and poking, survival being uppermost in his mind. Trott felt the same, and they must both have been relieved to see Richardson walk from the field, exhausted by his illness.

Harry Trott suddenly went after Peel, but merely edged him into Gay's gloves: 45 for 2. That brought in young left-handed Darling, on a 'king pair'. He was soon into his stride, though he needed to resist Briggs's derisory high-floating teasers, and by the end of the fifth day Australia were steady again and well on course to making the formality requirement of 177: 113 for 2, Darling 44, Giffen, hampered by a blow on the knee from Lockwood, 30.

SIXTH DAY

As one contented Australian put it, it was 'a guinea to a gooseberry on Australia' to win: only 64 more needed, wise old Giffen and the brilliant youngster Darling in harness, and, if needed, Iredale (81 in the first innings) and Gregory (201) to follow, plus the two allrounders; Richardson was still below par, and all the other England bowlers had so far managed only six wickets between them in almost 200 overs. The Australian cricketers went down to breakfast at the Baden Baden Hotel, Coogee with great anticipation.

'It's all right, boys. The weather is beautiful!' roared Ernie Jones, who was first out of bed that morning.

England return from the field at Sydney—probably *not* at the end of the first Test, since only just over 1000 people were present to witness the stunning conclusion.

Giffen was confident too as he looked through the window at the bright blue sky—until he bumped into his skipper. Blackham, who had worried about the weather throughout the previous day, had a face 'long as a coffee-pot', and forecast bad things as they took off for the SCG, the carriage leaving deep furrows in the soft ground. It had rained heavily during the night. The uncovered pitch was saturated, transformed into a batsman's nightmare.

Some of Stoddart's men, feeling the match was lost, had got drunk on the Wednesday night, and it now fell to the captain to get the booziest of them all, Bobby Peel, sobered up for action. He was put under a cold shower and told of the duty which lay before him now that a blazing sun on the wet pitch had given England an unexpected opportunity to fight back for a victory which had seemed utterly impossible for the previous few days. Peel, as oblivious as any to the night's rainfall, at first thought somebody must have watered the wicket. As it gradually dawned on his befuddled brain that England were back in with a chance, he is supposed to have said to his skipper: 'Give me the ball, Mr Stoddart, and I'll get t'boogers out before loonch!'

In his fresh excitement, the sandy-haired Yorkshireman forgot the lingering discomfort which was the legacy of the extraction of five teeth just before the Test match.

With the late arrival of Lockwood as well as Peel, the start was delayed slightly, with Blackham's generous forbearance, the pitch becoming more glutinous with every minute. How the tabloid newspapers of today would have relished such a story: TEST DELAYED WHILE ENGLAND BOWLER SOBERED UP.

Stoddart placed a close-up field and entrusted Peel and Richardson with the first few overs. Under 2000 people were present, making the SCG seem like 'some silent cemetery' after the previous five days of large crowds and incessant applause. For the first time, a match had entered a sixth day.

Peel beat Giffen and Gay whipped off the bails, but the Australian had his back foot firmly anchored behind the crease. The Yorkshireman, despite his aching head, was pitching a perfect length, spinning widely and variously and getting spiteful lift. Richardson too was making the ball leap, only at a disconcerting pace.

Giffen edged a four from one which kept low, and Darling, recognising the dangers, bravely hit Peel out towards long-on and over the fence for a five. Bucketfuls of extra sawdust were brought to the middle and almost every ball saw the batsman walking out to pat down the disturbance in the muddy pitch.

With 53 to his name, and hero status his for a further hour or less of successful hitting, Joe Darling went after Peel again, lofted the ball into the deep, and saw Brockwell race in from in front of the two-and-sixpenny seats to cling to a very important catch.

News of the dramatic circumstances had swept across Sydney, and cabs and carriages were now being pulled at the gallop across Moore Park. Some of the latecomers were in time to see Giffen survive an lbw shout from Peel and then a catch to point off the same bowler, Brown's movement hampered by the wet turf. It made little difference, for Giffen was lbw to Briggs's first ball, slipping as he played at it: 135 for 4, last man 41; 42 needed.

The tall Iredale and the short Gregory tried, with nimble footwork, to get to the pitch of each ball, and another dozen runs came, with England experiencing some concern when Gay had a finger dislocated. The odds were still on an Australian win.

But Briggs lured Iredale into getting under a ball which climbed high before dropping into the bowler's grateful hands: 147 for 5. Surely Gregory, the first-innings double-century hero, would see Australia home? He had moved on to 16 when, trying to run Peel backward of point, he touched the ball into Gay's gloves: 158 for 6: 19 only now wanted.

MacLaren, at second slip, dropped Reedman, but the miss was not costly, for the South Australian now stepped out to Peel and missed. Leslie Gay had yet another accident, failing to take the ball cleanly; but his luck was in this time: it rebounded from his chest and broke the wicket. For ever more it would show in the book as 'st Gay b Peel'.

The slightly neurotic Blackham was now striding up and down the small players' balcony muttering 'Cruel luck' over and over. Behind him stood a stunned Giffen, singlet and shirt in hand, and

Lyons, sighing at what might have been had his innings not ended so abruptly the evening before, and Harry Graham, head in hands, a helpless twelfth man who had once survived for two hours against Peel on a wet pitch.

Still, Charlie Turner knew a thing or two about batting and could still carry Australia home with a few well-struck hits. He made two runs, but with 16 still needed, he hit a catch to Briggs at cover off Peel. The excitable little fieldsman, who only minutes before had been nodding his head and clicking his tongue after MacLaren's fielding error, was greatly elated by his own catch.

Ernie Jones now had a go at finishing the match with some hard hitting on this near-impossible pitch, but with only a single to his name he belted Briggs back over his head only to be caught by MacLaren. Nine down for 162; 15 needed; Blackham, with his painful thumb bandaged, walking mournfully to the crease to join Charlie McLeod.

The two slow left-armers have almost completed the job for England. Will their nerves hold? Will the fielders be up to the task if catches go flying? The ball is dispatched unerringly towards off stump. McLeod spars; takes a single. Stoddart peers anxiously around the field, at the batsmen's rigid countenances, at Peel's round face, so recently florid with alcohol.

Blackham pokes his bat forward and winces at the pain in his hand. Gay, fearful of letting through byes, gets his gloves over-deliberately in line. The ball spits from the treacherous surface.

Four of the 15 runs are banked. Then Peel bobs in again and drops the ball on a length. Bearded Blackham pushes out at it. It comes back towards the bowler. England, 261 behind on first innings, can now win the match if the resurrected Peel pockets the catch. He does. England have won by 10 runs, two minutes before lunch on the sixth day. They have won a match seemingly impossible to win.

The players were cheered generously as they filed back into the pavilion, and the congratulations came from all quarters. Over lunch, Phil Sheridan of the SCG Trust (whose tour guarantee was already covered), proposed a warm toast to the English team and its captain, who in turn spoke appreciatively of his players, who were, he repeated, a 'team of triers'. He freely acknowledged that the elements had suddenly given England a chance, but felt that much credit was still due to Peel (6 for 67) and Briggs (3 for 25) for taking full advantage. He congratulated the Australians on the manner in which they had taken their shock defeat. But Stoddart was clearly moved by the efforts of his own men in this 'uphill' game. Typically, he came back generously on the matter of Australia's ill-fortune with the rain, acknowledging that the weather alone had robbed them of victory. 'There'll be a good deal said about this match,' he predicted. And he wasn't wrong.

Bad news was on its way for Walter Humphreys, who did not play in this—or any other—Test match: his brother George, who had also played for Sussex, died during the fifth day of this Test.

Meanwhile, down in the small Victorian township of Jeparit, on the very day that this thrilling Test drew to its muddy conclusion, with its new world record aggregate of runs (1514), Australia's first great statesman, Robert Gordon Menzies, had chosen this Alice-in-Wonderland day of cricket on which to be born.

The primitive SCG scoreboard displays the sensational final innings details.

FIRST TEST MATCH

Sydney Cricket Ground, December 14, 15, 17, 18, 19, 20, 1894
Toss: Australia
Debuts: Australia–J Darling, FA Iredale, E Jones, CE McLeod, JC Reedman
England–JT Brown, FGJ Ford, LH Gay, AC MacLaren
12th Men: H Graham (Aust) and H Philipson (Eng)
Umpires: C Bannerman and J Phillips
Attendances: 10,917, 24,120, 11,606, 8034, 6168, 1268. Total: 62,113 Receipts £2832
Close of play: 1st day Aust 5-346 (Gregory 85, Reedman 4); 2nd day Eng 3-130 (Ward
   67, Brockwell 18); 3rd day Eng 325 all out; 4th day Eng (2) 4-268 (Brockwell 20,
   Peel 9); 5th day Aust (2) 2-113 (Giffen 30, Darling 44).

AUSTRALIA
First Innings

				Second Innings		
JJ Lyons	b Richardson	1		b Richardson	25	
GHS Trott	b Richardson	12		c Gay b Peel	8	
G Giffen	c Ford b Brockwell	161		lbw b Briggs	41	
J Darling	b Richardson	0		c Brockwell b Peel	53	
FA Iredale	c Stoddart b Ford	81	(6)	c & b Briggs	5	
SE Gregory	c Peel b Stoddart	201	(5)	c Gay b Peel	16	
JC Reedman	c Ford b Peel	17		st Gay b Peel	4	
CE McLeod	b Richardson	15		not out	2	
CTB Turner	c Gay b Peel	1		c Briggs b Peel	2	
*†JM Blackham	b Richardson	74	(11)	c & b Peel	2	
E Jones	not out	11	(10)	c MacLaren b Briggs	1	
Extras	(b8, lb3, w1)	12		(b2, lb1, nb4)	7	
Total	(172.3 overs, 431 mins)	586		(68.0 overs, 198 mins)	166	

Fall: 10, 21, 21, 192, 331, 379, 400, 409, 563
26, 45, 130, 135, 147, 158, 159, 161, 162

BOWLING	O	M	R	W	w/nb		O	M	R	W	w/nb
Richardson	55.3	13	181	5	- -		11	3	27	1	- -
Peel	53	14	140	2	- -		30	9	67	6	- -
Briggs	25	4	96	0	- -	(4)	11	2	25	3	- -
Lockwood	3	2	1	0	- -	(3)	16	3	40	0	- 4
Brockwell	22	7	78	1	- -						
Ford	11	2	47	1	1 -						
Stoddart	3	0	31	1	- -						

ENGLAND
First Innings

			Second Innings	
AC MacLaren	c Reedman b Turner	4	b Giffen	20
A Ward	c Iredale b Turner	75	b Giffen	117
*AE Stoddart	c Jones b Giffen	12	c Giffen b Turner	36
JT Brown	run out (Lyons/Blackham)	22	c Jones b Giffen	53
W Brockwell	c Blackham b Jones	49	b Jones	37
R Peel	c Gregory b Giffen	4	b Giffen	17
FGJ Ford	st Blackham b Giffen	30	c & b McLeod	48
J Briggs	b Giffen	57	b McLeod	42
WH Lockwood	c Giffen b Trott	18	b Trott	29
†LH Gay	c Gregory b Reedman	33	b Trott	4
T Richardson	not out	0	not out	12
Extras	(b17, lb3, w1)	21	(b14, lb8)	22
Total	(140.3 overs, 344 mins)	325	(181.4 overs, 412 mins)	437

Fall: 14, 43, 78, 149, 155, 211, 211, 252, 325
44, 115, 217, 245, 290, 296, 385, 398, 420

BOWLING	O	M	R	W	w/nb		O	M	R	W	w/nb
Jones	19	7	44	1	1 -		19	0	57	1	- -
Turner	44	16	89	2	- -		35	14	78	1	- -
Giffen	43	17	75	4	- -		75	25	164	4	- -
Trott	15	4	59	1	- -		12.4	2	22	2	- -
McLeod	14	2	25	0	- -		30	7	67	2	- -
Reedman	3.3	1	12	1	- -		6	1	12	0	- -
Lyons	2	2	0	0	- -		2	0	12	0	- -
Iredale							2	1	3	0	- -

ENGLAND WON BY 10 RUNS

CHAPTER EIGHT

A Short Breather

The newspapers, sole communicators–apart from word of mouth–of the dramatic events in the first Test match, lavished praise on England for their fightback and acknowledged, almost in awe, the fickleness of the weather. Some correspondents–who may never have had to bat on an Australian sticky against artful bowlers like Peel and Briggs–were even critical of Australia for making 420 runs fewer in the second innings than in the first.

'That's the match,' Briggs said when Blackham had won the toss, according to one of the cuttings in Stoddart's scrapbook. Peel, the report remarked, 'found the match rather a trying one, and came in fairly done up'. Did that particular reporter not know the truth?

Another cutting reveals that delighted though the Englishmen may have been, one at least could not resist the temptation to tease. They went off to the races, where one player stated gleefully that 'we like your climate immensely; it's so suited to the game, you know'. On the light blue (Australian) side 'feelings had to be concealed'.

And as the Victorian and South Australian players boarded the southbound express train, Jack Lyons said, 'Yes, we're going home. About time, isn't it?'

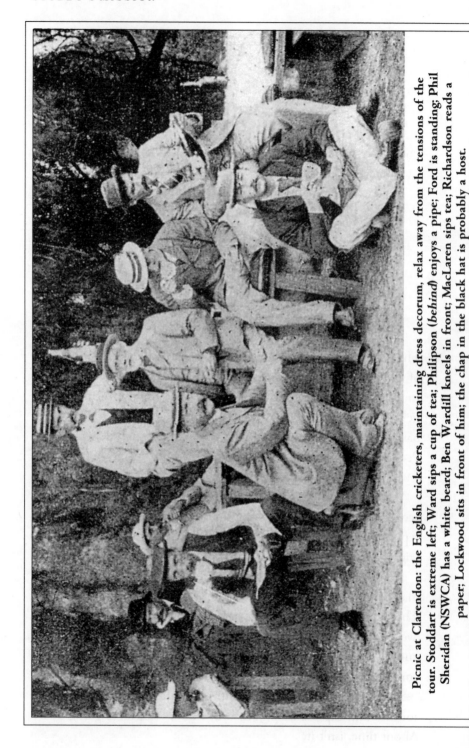

Picnic at Clarendon: the English cricketers, maintaining dress decorum, relax away from the tensions of the tour. Stoddart is extreme left; Ward sips a cup of tea; Philipson (*behind*) enjoys a pipe; Ford is standing; Phil Sheridan (NSWCA) has a white beard; Ben Wardill kneels in front; MacLaren sips tea; Richardson reads a paper; Lockwood sits in front of him; the chap in the black hat is probably a host.

Blackham declined to be interviewed.

Back at the Hotel Australia, where the English amateurs were staying, as Stoddart and his fellows entered the dining-room that evening, 200 diners cheered them loudly, the captain bowing in acknowledgment.

The next day, Friday, was free, before the English team played Eighteen Juniors of Sydney, again at the SCG, on the Saturday and Monday. We shall never know if the English bowlers over-celebrated after the Sydney Test victory, but they were anything but effective against the Juniors, who scored 327 for 7 on the first day, rising to 442 for 9 on the second before the captain had the satisfaction of signalling a declaration. By then, the 21-year-old Paddington allrounder and future Australian Test captain MA Noble was 152 not out. He then took the wickets of Ford and Stoddart as the tourists batted through to 151 for 6 and a lopsided draw.

Quite as significant as Noble's performance, however, was an 85-minute innings of 67 by a slender youth of 17 who was making his first appearance in the big-time. His style was described by the *Sydney Morning Herald* as 'superior'. He was once deceived by a Humphreys underarm legspinner. He gave no identifiable chance. He treated the bowling of these famous Englishmen with 'the greatest disrespect'. He would go on doing that for seasons to come, until his health failed him totally 20 years later. His name was Victor Thomas Trumper.

CHAPTER NINE

Second Test

Rain again. Would the second Test, at Melbourne, start on time? At least, there had not been enough 'liquid sunshine' to lay the dust which rose irritatingly in clouds from the road between the Jolimont gate and the grandstand and were borne by the north-westerly breeze into the members' reserve and grandstand enclosure.

The pitch, despite some tarpaulin covering, had absorbed a lot of rain. But it was deemed playable, the only cause of delay at the start being the Australians' last-minute huddle to choose a captain, Blackham, old and injured, having played his final Test. The matter ought to have been dealt with hours earlier, but such was the casual nature of procedure. As it was, George Giffen was elected, proposed by his only serious rival, Harry Trott.

AE Stoddart, meanwhile, had been seen in the pavilion, prowling around anxiously, and then out in the middle, pressing his hand into the pitch and leaving a damp imprint. When Giffen finally emerged from the Australian 'boudoir', asking 'Where's Stoddy?', the English captain was occupying a quiet spot, where Giffen found him. 'Let's look at that pitch, Stoddy, before we toss.'

It was said that you could tell batsmen from bowlers by the looks on their faces: ghoulish anticipation from the latter, apprehension from the former. The more thoughtful pundits were not so certain about bowling first, for difficult though the pitch might be after the rain, it might get even worse as it became used, even allowing for a rolling between innings. Tension was higher than usual.

Giffen examined the surface very closely and thought and thought, while Stoddart stood by, hands behind back. Then the coin went up, glittering in the sunlight, and Australia had the choice. Giffen strode off to confer with Trott and Bruce, who went to inspect a pitch that bore all the mystery of an unidentified reptile. It was eventually decided that England should be put in.

There were four changes among Australia's personnel. Blackham's place behind the stumps was taken by 'Affie' Jarvis, from South Australia; Reedman, Jones and McLeod were omitted; Hugh Trumble was available on his home ground; Billy Bruce, the slender left-hander, came in; and Arthur Coningham became the first Queensland player to be chosen for Australia. In the England ranks, with so little room for manoeuvre (they had only 13 on tour), Gay's wretched display behind the stumps let in Stoddart's great friend Hylton Philipson.

Also omitted was Humphreys, the father figure, who had wielded the carving knife across the roast beef at the team's Christmas dinner, the cricketers having strolled through Sydney's harbourside Botanical Gardens, as pleasing a place as any to pass Christmas Day, before the outing to Randwick Races on Boxing Day. Now it was down to business again, on a Melbourne Cricket Ground whose capacity and profile were similar to Sydney's. The pavilion, built in 1881 and extended in 1886, was a solid-looking two-storey construction, with an open seating terrace on the roof. Next to it was a long, imposing grandstand, with flags flying from its rounded rooftop, but no further structures of any substance disturbed the wide walkway and benches, fringed by elms and other trees, for almost 270 degrees. This took in 'The Pit', where the chatter was animated and often humorous, and a scoreboard slightly more informative than the one at Sydney. Then, beyond a high railing barrier, a wooden telegraph booth was alongside the ladies' stand, separated by yet another shady tree. The Southern Stand, with its vulgar Bay 13 contingent, and its successor, the Great Southern Stand, built at a cost of $145-million in time for the 1992 World Cup, were way in the future, as was just about every other feature of today's MCG. Here was the ground at its charming late-Victorian best.

The pitch was rolled after the toss, and soon Giffen was leading out the Australians, garbed in the dark blue colours of Victoria, cap and sash. The crowd was building up fast to an eventual 14,000, the seating area all spoken for some time before the delayed start.

Australia's supporters were well satisfied by the lunch interval, when England were 44 for the loss of five; and yet more euphoric when the last wicket fell at 75. Giffen, exploding the conviction that he was the most selfish of bowlers, denied himself a bowl in these favourable conditions. He used only Coningham, Turner and Trumble, and they did the job in 40 overs and one ball.

Arthur Coningham, the left-armer, ran in and bowled the first ball, which reared at MacLaren, who nudged up a catch to point, thus providing the first instance in the 43 Tests played until then of a wicket falling to the first ball of a Test. 'Conny' also became the first bowler to strike with his maiden delivery in Test cricket. He showed understandable pleasure, though it was later noted that he had 'lost much of his eccentric mannerism'. Melbourne was his native town, though he was now a Queenslander.

Stoddart joined Ward, and they watched the ball closely as it capered about off the soft turf. Having got the gist of things, Stoddart then began to hit over the top—until one from Turner crept through, under the England captain's pull stroke: 19 for 2. The 'Terror' had just hit him above the elbow, forcing an involuntary yell which was heard all round the MCG.

Brown was caught at slip by Trumble off Turner without scoring, and Brockwell also got a duck, hitting Coningham out to Iredale: 26 for 4. Only Albert Ward seemed to have any sort of chance of a longish life out there. His touch was clever, his nerve cool. 'Felix' (Horan) wrote: 'It is not easy, through the cold medium of print, to give you an adequate or just idea of the masterful manner

Stoddart, with a slightly self-conscious smile, tunes up in the nets at Melbourne, where he made a monumental 173.

The only known action shot of Charlie Turner, 'The Terror',
whose skills were repeatedly of value to Australia—not least in
the second Test—until his shock omission on the eve of the
climactic Test.

Tom Richardson, England's titanic fast bowler, who
destroyed Australia's first innings at Melbourne, and went on
to bag 32 wickets in the series.

in which he negotiated high balls, breakbacks, low balls, balls that talk to you, balls that won't say anything to you, etc. Suffice it to say that at luncheon time, when he fell caught by Darling at third man off Hugh Trumble, he had made 30 out of 44 for 5 wickets. As Stoddart made 10 of the 44 you won't take long to make out what the remaining three made, especially when I tell you that there were four sundries.'

One policeman stood watch beside the pitch during the gossipy lunch-break, as if the pitch were a piece of criminal evidence.

Peel, 0 not out after 20 minutes, hit Turner through the air for four but was then caught at slip; Ford, having cut Turner to the fence, was caught high at slip off the lanky Trumble the ball after being let off by Trott, a sharp chance at point. Briggs cut his first ball for four, was aghast when the umpire signalled leg-byes from what he felt was a touch, saw Trumble spoil a difficult caught-and-bowled chance, and was then caught on the leg side off Turner. Philipson was quickly held in the deep, as was Richardson, for the fourth duck of the innings, leaving Lockwood, who had used his pads liberally, 3 not out. England 75 all out in just under two hours, Turner 5 for 32, Trumble 3 for 15, Coningham 2 for 17. Now it was Australia's turn. Giffen ordered the heavy roller.

The pitch was easing but still much favoured bowlers, and when Australia's first three batsmen were out for 15, it began to look like a struggle for first-innings advantage, and a shortish sort of match. Richardson bowled Lyons with a fast offcutter; Bruce, missed by Brockwell at slip off Richardson, top-edged Peel to slip; and Gregory, fresh from his double-century at Sydney, made only 2 before slicing Richardson to third man.

Giffen and Darling, who each made 32, added 38 brave runs for the fourth wicket in 30 minutes, left-hander Darling hitting Lockwood over the pickets for a five before the Surrey paceman yorked him with his cunning slow ball: 53 for 4.

With Iredale as his companion, Giffen eased Australia past England's 75 with a series of firm drives, before Richardson hit him painfully on the knee, and then bowled Iredale. Giffen went soon afterwards, neatly caught by keeper Philipson down the leg side off Briggs, and it was 86 for 6. The captain's exemplary innings had lasted 95 minutes and was chanceless.

Coningham tried dashing out at Richardson's sharp pace and somehow gathered 10 before, with the 100 safely posted, he nicked the fast bowler to Philipson, standing no more than 10 yards back, the ball being slowed by the soft pitch. Richardson took his fifth wicket by bowling Trumble. Trott (16 in 52 minutes) now got himself run out against Jarvis's call, Peel at mid-off tossing the ball back to the bowler. And with the total 123, 48 ahead of England, the last wicket fell, ending the 2½-hour innings. Australians generally felt disappointment, for conditions were not so bad now. Care such as Giffen and Trott had displayed might have reduced the damage, and after the Sunday of rest, the pitch may well have rolled out firm and true and allowed Australia to build up a match-winning total. Instead, after the sensational first couple of hours on this opening day, the match was on a fairly even keel, thanks as much as anything to Tom Richardson's sustained effort. His whole manner reminded 'Felix' of Spofforth; there could be no greater compliment.

SECOND DAY

New Year's Eve dawned grey and cool but brightened significantly. By prior arrangement, the pitch had been mowed and rolled and the outfield cut, and it was soon clear that batsmen need have no worries about the pitch. It was almost as if another Test match were starting.

MacLaren and Ward faced Coningham and Giffen, and the runs came. Turner knocked MacLaren's off stump out with his second ball, with 24 scored; but the solid Ward was joined by an unusually determined and cautious Stoddart, who broke from his watchfulness once in a while to punish anything off-line. With the arrears wiped off, Stoddart indulged himself in a huge on-drive off the threatening Turner, the ball bouncing onto the asphalt in front of the pavilion. A fielder was immediately sent out to long-on.

By lunch, England were 78 for 1, and everyone knew they meant business, especially Charlie Turner, whose fastish offbreaks had been well-directed. Resuming, England moved to 101 before

Pathways of anticipation: the approach–trodden by the eager
thousands–to the Melbourne Cricket Ground.

'Second Test Match on the Melbourne Cricket Club Ground
between Mr Stoddart's Team and the Australian Eleven'.
Around 65,000 attended this one.

Ward was unexpectedly out, bowled off his pads by Turner for 41. Brown replaced him, 'a sound batsman without polish, and good in most strokes, except hard, straight-ahead hits' according to 'Felix'.

Drewy Stoddart, however, was the centre of attraction. MacLaren best illustrated his aura that day: 'It was one of those days when he convinced you from the commencement of his innings that nothing could get past his bat, that there was no ball that could not be hit to the exact spot he selected.'

He slowed down in the seventies, but for all the mixed skills of Turner and Trumble, Giffen and Coningham, and Trott's legbreaks, he remained in charge, an undemonstrative, easy-moving, athletic figure. Brown helped him add 90 in only 65 minutes before left-armer Bruce had the Yorkshireman caught behind. At tea Stoddart was 95.

The century came, his second against Australia, with a legside boundary off Australia's greatest bowler, Turner. It had taken him 170 minutes—slow by his standards—but was, by his own declaration, 'the century of my career'. And he made a few. 'Nothing I have ever done in cricket,' he later stated, 'gives me the same lasting pleasure to look back on as that innings', which he explained away merrily on another occasion by saying, 'I had to buck up for England, home and beauty.'

He was not finished yet by a long way. Brockwell, who sometimes looked 'more the soldier than batsman' at the crease, though he reminded some Australians of Murdoch, kept Stoddart good company, making two runs to his one in a fourth-wicket stand of 31. The Surrey man was starting to look confident, tugging at his cap. It was a relief to Australia when he chopped Turner into his stumps.

Stoddart went into his shell for the remaining time, and Peel knew that any rashness on his part would deeply disappoint his skipper. They played out time for a reasonably secure 287 for 4, Stoddart 151, Peel 18 in 78 watchful minutes. It would have been a lot more had not Harry Trott been almost impassable at point to Stoddart's crisp square-cuts. All the Australians had fielded well, apart from the carthorse Lyons and the over-excitable Coningham.

THIRD DAY

The New Year's Day holiday found over 20,000 people packing the MCG to see if Giffen and his men could hold onto this Test and avoid going two down. The crush at Richmond railway station an hour before the start was memorable, and the hordes who stepped through Yarra Park found it no easy job to weave their way across the Jolimont approach, packed solid with horse-drawn cabs. Flemington Races may have been a serious counter-attraction, but most of the world wanted to be part of the England v Australia Test match.

In the first 50 minutes only 33 runs were added against probing bowling. It was extremely serious stuff, with Giffen and Turner straining for the breakthrough.

It came without warning. Stoddart had unwrapped a couple of boundary shots and seemed in line to make a double-century when Giffen's faster ball found the stumps via an edge: 320 for 5, England 272 ahead, Stoddart 173, compiled in five hours 20 minutes, with 14 fours and one five, plus two other fives, all-run. He gave no distinct chance, and seemed as fresh as when he started as he returned to the deep chorus of admiration from all round the ground and disappeared into the shadows of the pavilion. It was England's highest innings against Australia, beating WG Grace's 170 at The Oval in 1886, and was to remain the highest by an England captain in a Test in Australia from the inception of Test cricket in 1877 until almost 100 years later, when Mike Denness scored 188 on this same ground in 1975.

Peel and Ford took the score to 350 for 5 at the luncheon adjournment but afterwards the Middlesex man—'Six-foot-two of don't care'—was caught by Trott at point, and the crowd licked its lips when Briggs skipped out to the middle. His antics never failed to amuse. At 383 he lost Peel, who was stumped off Giffen for a 2¼-hour 53 which contained not one boundary, one of his most valuable Test contributions. Briggs continued to ride his luck. Iredale got his left hand to one chance, and Gregory, deep at square leg, fluffed another. Giffen, though, fired a full-toss through Briggs's crossbat to get him lbw just after the 400 had been raised. The end was in sight.

Or was it? Australia—without Turner, who had ricked his back—had to bowl away while an infuriating 53 runs came from the ninth-wicket partnership of Lockwood and Philipson. Giffen, moving towards the end of a marathon effort of 470 balls, missed a whistling return catch from Lockwood, but from 0 for 100 he finished with 6 for 155, trimming Philipson's bails and having Richardson caught by Gregory near the fence after misjudging the flight of the catch and holding the rebound from his left hand. England 475 all out (all 11 batsmen reaching double figures—for the first time in a Test), 400 more than their first innings; Australia 428 for a series-levelling victory. When Bruce and Trott took everything that came their way in the remaining 78 minutes, making 43 each, Australia were looking at a target of 342 with a fresh start tomorrow. It was looking like another classic.

FOURTH DAY

On the Wednesday the score rose to 98, when Billy Bruce (54) had the misfortune to stub his bat into the turf as he drove at Peel, and Stoddart took the catch at mid-off. The prematurely grey Giffen, his 78.2 overs pushed into memory already, now planned a long, long innings, and at lunch he was well satisfied with 149 on the board, nine wickets in hand, Trott 63 and perhaps less hungry for having swallowed a fly on this stifling hot day, Giffen 28 and looking ominously secure.

The total grew: 186 for 1, almost halfway, and the pitch still playing well. Then Stoddart called Brockwell into the attack, and the Surrey allrounder swung the match with three quick wickets: Giffen, playing to leg, spooned a catch to cover; Trott, five short of his century, cracked one back at the bowler, who swooped to hold the catch; and Darling failed to handle one which pitched in line with his leg stump and hit the off. Now it was 214 for 4, and soon 216 for 5 as Richardson broke through Gregory's defences. The ground had gone quiet. Australia's dream seemed shattered.

From 231 for 5 at the 4 o'clock interval, Lyons, his entry delayed to No. 7 at his own request, pushed the total to 241 before

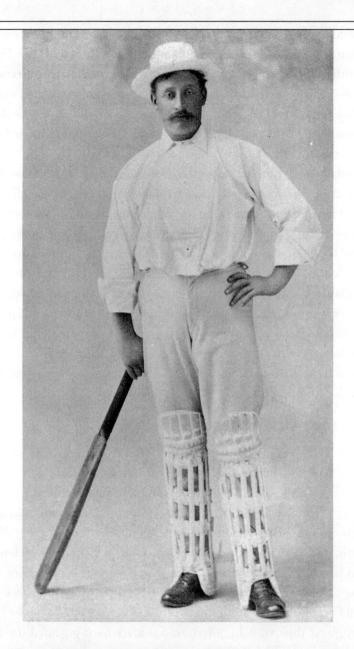

The genial Harry Trott, who just missed out on a century in
the second Test, at Melbourne. He contributed something
worthwhile to Australia's cause with bat, ball or in the field
in almost every Test.

thin-edging a typically robust hit against Peel into his stumps. Richardson bowled Jarvis and Coningham was bowled by Peel. Trumble was run out to a close decision which would have warranted a video replay a century later. And one wicket was left, Turner having joined Iredale, who was batting as soundly as his English counterpart Ward had done. Turner was almost bowled first ball, but serious frustration for England now followed.

Iredale and Turner stopped the flow of spectators from the ground as the clock-hands ticked from 5 pm towards the closure at 6. They dealt with anything the Englishmen could bowl at them, and so het-up did the volatile Lockwood become at one point that when he fielded and threw, and the ball struck Turner's bat, he appealed for 'obstructing the field'. Umpire Jim Phillips dealt with the matter firmly enough by stating that 'over' had been called, but Turner was not amused at the aspersion on his sportsmanship.

The 10th-wicket pair were still together at the close—328 for 9, 100 still needed for victory—Iredale 63, Turner (whose career included two first-class centuries) 26. Their defiance almost deserved a week of non-stop rain.

FIFTH DAY

About 1500 people turned up, free of charge (takings of almost £3000 had put the anxious Melbourne Cricket Club finances on a relieved footing), to see what Iredale and Turner could make of the desperate position, and after an over from Richardson from the pavilion end, Peel's first ball was straight, characteristically on a length, and kept low enough to breach the tall Iredale's defence. Stoddart had certainly addressed his bowler—this time not so hungover as at Sydney—'with the little touch of humour which would put Bobby into the frame of mind'.

England thus won by 94 runs, Stoddart having gained, in the words of the *Pall Mall Gazette*, honours not so much international as immortal. His innings of 173 remains one of the best in Anglo-Australian combat, but his stewardship of his players was also a crucial factor. One of them, Brockwell, was presented with the ball with which he had that decisive spell of 3 for 9—Trott, Giffen and

Darling. In response to someone's loud urging during the presentation lunch in the MCG pavilion, the chairman tossed the ball to Brockwell, who caught it smoothly with one hand. Everything was going England's way. It will never be known whether George Giffen, in his speech of response, truly believed it when he said that the Australians could still produce a superior team.

As at Sydney, had the outcome of the toss mattered? Perhaps it was as well that Stoddart had lost again, initially disappointing the two Anglo-Indian girls who had sent him—or delivered—a lucky token in Sydney on Christmas Day, hoping he would win the toss in the next Test.

A long way removed from the MCG scoreboard of today, the telegraph of 1894-95 shows the sorry tale for Australia at the end of the second Test.

SECOND TEST MATCH

Melbourne Cricket Ground, December 29, 31, 1894, January 1, 2, 3, 1895
Toss: Australia
Debuts: Australia– A Coningham
12th Men: J Harry (Aust). No 12th named for Eng
Umpires: T Flynn and J Phillips
Attendances: 14,000, 15,000, 21,000, 14,000, 1500. Total: About 65,000
Receipts: £2879
Close of play: 1st day Aust 123 all out; 2nd day Eng (2) 4-287 (Stoddart 151, Peel 18); 3rd day Aust (2) 0-86 (Bruce 43, Trott 43); 4th day Aust (2) 9-328 (Iredale 63, Turner 26).

ENGLAND
First Innings

				Second Innings	
AC MacLaren	c Trott b Coningham	0		b Turner	15
A. Ward	c Darling b Trumble	30		b Turner	41
*AE Stoddart	b Turner	10		b Giffen	173
JT Brown	c Trumble b Turner	0		c Jarvis b Bruce	37
W Brockwell	c Iredale b Coningham	0		b Turner	21
R Peel	c Trumble b Turner	6		st Jarvis b Giffen	53
FGJ Ford	c Giffen b Trumble	9		c Trott b Giffen	24
WH Lockwood	not out	3	(9)	not out	33
J Briggs	c Bruce b Turner	5	(8)	lbw b Giffen	31
†H Philipson	c Darling b Turner	1		b Giffen	30
T Richardson	c Iredale b Trumble	0		c Gregory b Giffen	11
Extras	(lb9, nb2)	11		(b1, lb2, nb3)	6
Total	(40.1 overs, 115 mins)	75		(202.2 overs, 477mins)	475

Fall: 0, 19, 23, 26, 44, 58, 60, 70, 71

24, 101, 191, 222, 320, 362, 383, 402, 455

BOWLING	O	M	R	W	w/nb		O	M	R	W	w/nb
Coningham	11	5	17	2	- -		20	4	59	0	- -
Turner	20	9	32	5	- -	(3)	55	21	99	3	- -
Trumble	9.1	4	15	3	- 2	(5)	26	6	72	0	- 3
Giffen						(2)	78.2	21	155	6	- -
Trott						(4)	17	0	60	0	- -
Bruce							4	0	21	1	- -
Lyons							2	1	3	0	- -

AUSTRALIA
First Innings

				Second Innings	
JJ Lyons	b Richardson	2	(7)	b Peel	14
W Bruce	c Ford b Peel	4	(1)	c Stoddart b Peel	54
*G Giffen	c Philipson b Briggs	32		c Brown b Brockwell	43
SE Gregory	c Ward b Richardson	2		b Richardson	12
J Darling	b Lockwood	32		b Brockwell	5
FA Iredale	b Richardson	10		b Peel	68
GHS Trott	run out (Peel/Richardson)	16	(2)	c & b Brockwell	95
A Coningham	c Philipson b Richardson	10	(9)	b Peel	3
H Trumble	b Richardson	1	(10)	run out (Briggs/Philipson)	2
†AH Jarvis	c Brown b Briggs	11	(8)	b Richardson	4
CTB Turner	not out	1		not out	26
Extras	(w2)	2		(b5, lb1, nb1)	7
Total	(55.5 overs, 150 mins)	123		(136.1 overs, 366 mins)	333

Fall: 4, 12, 15, 53, 80, 86, 108, 110, 116

98, 191, 206, 214, 216, 241, 254, 263, 268

BOWLING	O	M	R	W	w/nb		O	M	R	W	w/nb
Richardson	23	6	57	5	1 -		40	10	100	2	- -
Peel	14	4	21	1	- -		40.1	9	77	4	- -
Lockwood	5	0	17	1	1 -		25	5	60	0	- 1
Briggs	13.5	2	26	2	- -		12	0	49	0	- -
Ford							5	2	7	0	- -
Brockwell							14	3	33	3	- -

ENGLAND WON BY 94 RUNS

CHAPTER TEN

Third Test

Stoddart and his men played a two-day match in Ballarat on their way to Adelaide for the third Test match. On the Saturday they scored 187 against the Eighteen of Victoria's 'Golden City', Jack Brown bulking up the innings with 64, Albert Ward making a duck when it hardly mattered. On the Sunday, having been down the Last Chance mine the previous day, there was little else for them to do but to wander round the more beautiful parts of Ballarat, including the Botanical Gardens and the lake, while several of the English cricketers went riding. Leslie Gay's horse ran off with him and tossed him to the ground, but no limbs were broken. On Monday the match was resumed, and Walter Humphreys, shirtsleeves flapping distractingly, took 10 for 51 as the locals' 17 wickets mustered 103, and second time round the visitors scored 149 for 7, Johnny Briggs completing a 'pair'.

Safely transported to Adelaide, the Englishmen went down to the Oval to watch the closing stages of the Sheffield Shield match in which South Australia beat New South Wales on the fourth day by four wickets, Giffen taking a Shield record 16 for 186 to go with his current Shield batting record (205) and innings bowling record (9 for 147). His stamina would have ensured him of a lucrative endorsement contract of some sort in modern times.

Seven of the Australian XI which had just lost the second Test took part in this match, and when it was over, the English team had a net. Stoddart may have wondered if a place should be found for his lob bowler in the Adelaide Test, but resisted the thought. Humphreys was good at mopping up the minor opposition and making those matches easier, but he would stick to the same side which won for him in Melbourne.

Australia, in contrast, made four changes. Lyons had flu and was out of form, and Trumble, Coningham and Turner were omitted, Turner the surprise. He was made twelfth man midst murmurs of personality clashes. Stoddart would have been elated at the news. Meanwhile, the English captain declined all invitations. Now was the time to rest and prepare to complete the mission with a third straight win.

Australia's four newcomers were Syd Callaway, whose bowling for NSW had just accounted for seven wickets in the Shield match; and the Victorians, Jack Harry and Jack Worrall, who must have impressed Giffen in the Shield match at Adelaide a few weeks earlier; plus the younger brother of Harry Trott, Albert, keen, talented, unpredictable.

It was an Adelaide Oval not all that dissimilar to today's ground, uncluttered, leisurely, long on the drive, narrow both sides, usually a batsman's dream, with a big, blue sky above, the ranges in the distance, and the stately St Peter's Cathedral just beyond the long-leg boundary. In 1895 the scoreboard was primitive but informative, its ornate replacement not to be built until 1911. The gable-roofed grandstand down one side was later to be extended, and one day Giffen's name would be perpetuated upon it. And for this big match, a large marquee had been erected on Australia's third Test match ground. Within 100 years, the striking Sir Donald Bradman Stand would be built, but in 1895. The Don's first appearance on the ground was still 33 years in the future. And as for the Vic Richardson Gates, this greatest of Adelaide sportsmen, grandfather of the Chappells, was a four-month-old in swaddling clothes when this third Test of the 1894-95 series was staged.

The heat was killing: 100 degrees Fahrenheit in the shade, 155 in the middle—though Stoddart has scribbled '108 in shade 166 in sun' in his scrapbook. It was a day for winning the toss. Giffen did.

Firstly the Australians had to go through the time-consuming process of electing a captain, and the local legend held his position. Then he had to find his opposing skipper. Stoddart was chatting with some of his players under a tree at the back of the pavilion, and Giffen borrowed a shilling coin from one of them, Richardson, for the toss, keeping it afterwards as a souvenir of his luck. The wicket was so hard that Lockwood had glided across it, saying, 'Why, it's good enough for skating!'

There were almost 6000 present when Stoddart led out his men at 12.15 pm, followed by the Australian openers, Harry Trott and Billy Bruce, who wore the yellow-and-black colours of the local cricket authority. Richardson and Peel awaited them, as contrasting a pair of opening bowlers as Test cricket has ever seen. And after five minutes, Australia had 22 on the board. Bruce then offered a chance to MacLaren on the leg boundary, unaccepted, but soon played on to Richardson: 31 for 1.

In strode the revered Giffen, Australia's cricket king, on the ground he had turned into his own private playground. The reception was inspiring. At first, Trott made the running, hitting ball after ball across the rough outfield to the asphalt cycle-track, raising the total to 69. Then a run-out tragedy let England back into the game. Peel hit Trott's pad and there was an lbw appeal. While all else was frozen into a dramatic tableau, Giffen saw a quick single there and dashed down the pitch. Harry Trott didn't but heroically stepped out of his crease by way of sacrifice. His 48 (in only 50 minutes) included eight fours, taming Peel and Richardson as he progressed.

The fast bowler was rested, remarking, 'If I have to bowl much more, by the time we have to bat the wicket will be real sticky'—so much sweat had he sprayed about him. Now it was Brockwell's turn to impress again with a tight length and just enough work on the ball. By lunch, Australia were 80 for 2, and Ernie Jones, who was not wanted by Australia in this match, cheerfully warned the

A little fraternisation at the net practice: Jim Phillips,
England's Australian-born umpire, Albert Ward, Tom
Richardson, Jack Brown, and Frank Iredale.

Adelaide Oval 100 years ago. Here the Australian fightback began.

Australia's squad for the third Test, at Adelaide, where a victory was vital if the series was to be kept alive. *Standing:* ST Callaway, W Bruce, J Harry, FA Iredale, GHG Searcy (umpire); *seated:* GHS Trott, CTB Turner, J Worrall, G Giffen, J Darling, AH Jarvis; *in front:* SE Gregory, AE Trott.

red-faced Englishmen that it would get twice as hot during the afternoon.

Richardson soon made another breakthrough, beating Iredale for speed, and it was South Australia at the wicket as Joe Darling, sleeves rolled up, joined his captain, Giffen. Richardson thundered in again and hurled a yorker at Darling, trying for a repetition of his Sydney dismissal. The left-hander dug it out. A tough period followed as England worked hard to escape a long sentence under the lethal sun. Peel developed a slight ankle sprain, and Briggs tried his luck. And just after the 100 had been raised, Darling swished twice, three times, four times at Briggs, finally skying the ball for wicketkeeper Philipson to accept the catch, which will have pleased also the Toorak heiress, daughter of a well-known stock salesman, to whom, it was whispered, the Englishman had recently become engaged.

A full-scale Australian middle-order collapse now developed. Richardson powered in and had Gregory cutting without full control, Brown holding the catch at point. Then he crashed one through Jack Harry's defence, and was soon throwing in from cover to run out Worrall before he had scored. It was a close decision, verified by those square-on in the Press-box, as well as by a German spectator who asserted: 'Vell, you know, I tink not he never ket pack to de chollik mark!'

It was a shameful exhibition on this beautiful pitch: 137 for 7, and the Englishmen now less conscious of the flies, which never let up.

Giffen, who had been troubled in the past by Richardson's pace, bounce and breakback, was coping well with him, and reached a worthy fifty with a 'pretty' (favourite word of the times) hit to leg for three. Richardson left the field with exhaustion, and Lockwood took over, almost immediately taking a return catch from Jarvis on the stroke of tea.

It was around this time that Sir John Downer, former Premier of South Australia, popped into the match and sat beside Albert Trott, who was padded up as next man in, but shaking with nerves, teeth chattering. 'What on earth's the matter with you, young fellow?' enquired the kindly, well-dressed gentleman. 'I'm in next, sir. It's my first Test match. I'm scared stiff!' Sir John then allegedly said, 'Don't be so silly. They'll never get you out!' How close he was to the truth.

Giffen, having outstayed eight partners, was out soon after the 15-minute interval, giving Brockwell a deserved wicket when he lifted one to deep mid-on. His 58 had taken 155 minutes and was chanceless, apart from a possible edge in the keeper's direction before he had scored, according to some of the fielders. Giffen had placed a cool towel around his head throughout the tea break and was heard to say, 'I have never felt so fatigued in all my life.' He also lamented the loss of Harry Trott, who could have made England suffer on such a day as this. Now, with Trott's younger brother as his partner, he showed how little faith he had in him by lifting his drive into Lockwood's hands. It was ironic, for Trott junior was to prove one of the hardest Australians to dismiss in this and the next Test.

Was it or was it not a good pitch? 'It's not the best of wickets,' quoth Giffen, 'but there's no sting in the bowling worth mentioning, and—well, we should have helped ourselves.'

The last pair did. From 157 for 9, Trott and Callaway scored 81 runs to save Australia's face. And they did it boldly. Trott began with a five (six in today's coinage) off his toes off Lockwood, landing the ball in a buggy in the driveway beyond the embankment. Later he drove one straight and would have run six as Lockwood puffed after it, had Callaway been up to the exertion. They settled for five. Callaway cut successive balls from Lockwood for four, and the crowd began to cheer up.

Trott was nearly caught off Ford, a hit into the blue beyond, with the lumbering Richardson unable to get there in time, and the mercy of drinks was called for.

England were missing Peel, but Stoddart, a little belatedly, brought back Richardson, and in the Press-box wise old Humphreys remarked that 'Someone will be bowled now.' Callaway was bowled by a beauty, Richardson's fifth wicket. Eighty-one had been added in 70 minutes, and the pair were given a throaty welcome as they left the arena, Callaway 41, Albert Trott 38 not out, Australia 238.

MacLaren and Briggs gathered five runs in the 10 minutes left that evening.

SECOND DAY

Cloud did little to reduce the blistering heat, and most of the players, particularly the English, had a bad night behind them. There had been hours of sleeplessness, with sweat-soaked sheets and throbbing heads, flushed faces, unending tossing and turning. Stoddart was spotted in the hotel corridor in the early hours, having just taken his fourth shower-bath of the night.

He ordered the iron roller to be pulled only once up and down the pitch before play began, not wishing to break it up but merely to flatten it out. A huge crowd was gathering—building up to 12,000, twice that of the previous day—and even the military band played slow numbers so that the musicians could keep an eye on the cricket. The tempo of play was anything but slow. English wickets clattered throughout, to the accompaniment of a hot wind and swirling dust. Only later in the day did the weather finally ease up.

Albert Trott was given an over from the Cathedral end, and then Giffen, switching from the River Torrens end, and Callaway did the rest. They took five wickets each as England crashed for 124 to finish 114 behind.

Giffen was some time settling down, and conceded a few runs, but Callaway was right on target, and began with six maiden overs before bowling Briggs. The outgoing batsman did not necessarily help those to follow by quite audibly warning, 'You'll have to keep your eyes open: it's a funny wicket.'

Next, Brockwell, in at No. 3, also made a dozen before hitting Callaway high above mid-off only for Harry to leap and hold the catch one-handed. Ward, having made only 5, untypically hit out at Giffen and was taken nicely by Bruce at long-on to make it 49 for 3, and with only a single from the new batsman, Stoddart (who had scored 134 here at Adelaide three years ago in his only previous Test innings on the ground), it became 50 for 4 as the England captain parried a series of offbreaks from Giffen before being bowled by a straight ball. 'Here's that dear Mr Stoddart,' a woman was heard to say as he walked to the wicket. 'What a shame,' she now murmured, as white umbrellas danced about 'like demon toadstools in a Christmas pantomime' at his dismissal and shouts of 'Bravo, George!' led massive cheering.

When Callaway removed MacLaren's leg stump, the noise rose again. England lunched sickly at 56 for 5. Callaway, whose first 10 overs had yielded 10 runs, now had 3 for 14, and South Australian player Reedman patriotically gave him a rubdown while Blackham, also at the match, talked tactics with Giffen. They were not alone in fearing a compulsory follow-on by England. With this pitch promising further deterioration, and with memories still vibrant of England's comeback at Sydney in the first Test, it had to be a matter of consideration whether to give runs away to avert the follow-on.

Peel was bowled by Callaway right after the interval—64 for 6— but somehow Brown and Ford survived, the Yorkshiremen punishing Giffen quite severely. Together they made 47 before, at 111, Ford became the first of three batsmen to be caught athletically some way from the bat by Worrall, who had dropped him at 13. There was no doubting that his batsmen were following Stoddart's instructions to strive for every run and not to fall deliberately short of the follow-on figure.

Without addition, Lockwood was caught by Worrall, and 13 runs later Philipson hit Giffen into Gregory's safe hands in front of the smokers' pavilion. Richardson then drove Callaway only for Worrall to take another high catch, and England's misery was complete, 124 all out, victims of exhaustion as much as anything else. Brown was left 39 not out, defiant if not elegant or chanceless, while Giffen's 5 for 76 was upstaged by Callaway's 5 for 37, with 13 maidens in his 26.3 overs. Eight of the 10 wickets fell to the final ball of an over, and the Australian fielding had been right out of the top drawer, holding six catches, intercepting reliably, and often hitting the stumps with direct throws. There might not, after all, be a 3-nil whitewash.

The *Adelaide Advertiser* reported one amusing little exchange between Worrall and a boy who stood by the players' entrance: 'Now then, Jack, just you catch three of them Englishers out and make up fer yer bloomin' duck's egg!' Having carried out the instructions, the player found the youngster still by the gate as he came off, grinning broadly, and saying: 'Well done, Jack. Wot did I tell yer?'

While Charlie Checkett rolled the pitch during the tea interval, commenting that the wicket 'is looking wonderfully well; there is only one little spot and it is right back', Giffen ladled out oatmeal and lemon-water (Blackham's recipe) to his men, until Stoddart addressed his own subdued band with a rallying 'Come on, boys.'

They had something early to cheer them when Harry Trott played a ball from Peel into his stumps before a run had been scored. But Giffen joined Bruce and put on 44 in positive fashion before Ford held the Australian captain nimbly at slip, letting Frank Iredale in for a long and decisive innings. Bruce stayed with him while 98 were added, the left-hander scoring faster and more attractively, and pleasing the onlooking Blackham, who remarked that Bruce had taken a lot of persuading to take time off from his legal work to play in this Test. And he needed the runs to make his place safe.

He reached 80, and there was little time remaining, when he slapped a Briggs long-hop into Brockwell's waiting hands on the square-leg fence. His knock had lasted only 110 minutes, and he and Iredale had just taken 19 off a Lockwood over. A century had seemed certain. At last Stoddart ceased to resemble a model for a statue of Melancholy.

There was a further morsel of encouragement that evening when Darling played weakly at Lockwood and was caught behind, but at 145 for 4, Iredale a solid 31 and limping from a turned ankle, Australia were already 259 ahead.

THIRD DAY

A day of rest behind them, the players stepped out into cooler conditions, the inhuman heat of the previous week having abated. 'I can't help thinking,' wrote one reporter, 'that many failures of the first few days were attributable as much as anything else to the roasting weather, for want of sleep all night and iced drinks all day play up with the liver and the eyesight.'

There was another large attendance, banks and government offices having been shut for a half-holiday, and they were in a good humour in view of the match situation. Peel's dropping of a return catch from Iredale did nothing to damage the happy mood, and accident-prone Lockwood hurt his hand and left the field, bringing none other than Albert Trott on as a substitute, and rendering Stoddart's face melancholic once more. Philipson's error in flooring an edge by Gregory off Richardson worsened matters. Iredale reached his fifty, and the only complaint the spectators had was when Albert Trott completed a wonderful piece of fielding before Lockwood came back on.

Gregory, supposedly less at ease on Adelaide's faster pitch, reached 20 before a ball from Richardson cannoned from his leg into his stumps: 197 for 5. And England fought back some more when Richardson bowled Harry out of Test cricket soon after the Victorian had late-cut him sweetly for four. Worrall started with a similar shot, but Richardson manfully kept the pressure on, with Briggs curling the ball from the other end, first over then round the wicket. Iredale, moving into the eighties, was the big obstacle.

Worrall went next, misjudging against Briggs and spooning a catch; but Jarvis began hitting boundaries without delay, and Iredale moved towards his hundred. A back-cut off Brockwell seemed to give him the century, if they could scramble four. He and Jarvis sprinted as the crowd's roar swelled, and Iredale's hundred was made safe, in 190 minutes. It had surely secured Australia's position?

On the stroke of lunch, Jarvis—to his disbelief—was caught by Brown at point off Peel for 29, and Australia went in at 283 for 8, 'Jarvie' disconsolate at his dismissal, slowly shaking his head and saying, 'I was in great nick.'

By now the lead was 397, but there was nothing untoward about the pitch, and Giffen wanted a bigger advantage. Albert Trott went out with Iredale, determined to meet his skipper's request.

Frank Iredale: his century at Adelaide put Australia in a
commanding position.

**Australia (the kangaroo) and England (the lion) both suffered
in turn from extremes of weather during the series, the rain
sometimes rendering batting close to impossible and the
intense heat weakening cricketers' resolve.**

Iredale was seeing the ball large, and found the boundary a few more times, but Trott was extremely close to being run out when Ward's smart throw was taken one-handed by Peel, who whipped off the bails. Umpire Jim Phillips's high reputation saw to it that his 'not out' verdict was queried by no-one.

For 4½ hours Iredale had been batting when, at 140, he received the worst ball of the match, a chest-high full-toss from Peel. Trying to place it for his 18th four, the Sydney man lobbed a return catch, 'neither Peel nor Iredale being able to keep a serious face over such an unexpected conclusion'. It was 347 for 9, and Callaway joined Trott. They had put on an extraordinary 81 for the 10th wicket in the first innings. It would be more than the Englishmen could bear if something similar happened now. It did.

'By jingo, I wish we had him,' Giffen said of Trott the 'Australian baby'. But there was no real chance of the Victorian's moving across to South Australia. It seemed a feeler had already been put out for him on behalf of Sussex. And now he raised his market value further by adding 64 with Callaway for the last wicket, and again finishing not out, this time with 72. England's fielders had 'developed the art of foot fielding lately', and who could blame them? Few things are more disheartening than last-wicket stands when the deficit is already over 450.

Callaway left most of the runmaking to his truculent partner, and when Richardson was rewarded with his eighth wicket of the match when he breached Callaway's defence, young Albert had banked 110 runs in his first Test match, elder brother Harry marvelling, 'Who'd have thought the kid could do it?' His unbeaten 72 came in 90 minutes, with 11 fours. And now he fancied a bowl.

It was, of course, a Test without time-limit, so England could look at no refuge in a draw, even if the weather intervened. Five hundred and twenty-six was the target, and the Australians understandably anticipated victory.

MacLaren and Ward gave England an encouraging start, 50 coming in an hour or so, with a bonus of a dropped catch—by Harry Trott off a fierce MacLaren cut—which would have given Albert Trott his first Test wicket. But it soon came, the same batsman lofting him out to the safe hands of Iredale. And straightaway Trott split a stump in bowling Ward. Philipson came in as nightwatchman, and Giffen was too good for him too, leaving England 56 for 3 at the close, Stoddart still on 1, Brown 2, little hope left, and Brown still feeling the pain of a knock from Trott.

FOURTH DAY

No more than 1500 turned up on the Tuesday to see the expected Australian victory, but those who were there felt they might have the additional delight of a top Stoddart innings, especially when he drove Trott the length of Adelaide Oval. But the captain reverted to extreme watchfulness, and was to spend 100 minutes over his 34 not out by the time his troops were all vanquished.

Brown went first, playing on to the irresistible Trott, who then had Stoddart dropped by Giffen at slip. Brockwell tried to gain some sort of initiative, but at 24 he hit one hard back at Trott, who parried the ball with one hand and clasped the rebound. Peel then bagged his 'pair' by returning the softest of catches to Trott: 102 for 6. Two more wickets fell at 128, Ford, having landed a ball from Giffen into the members' pavilion, between two defenceless ladies, was caught by Harry Trott off his brother, and Briggs was bowled by Trott for nought, and lucky to make that. Lockwood let rip, only to see Iredale run hard for the catch and secure it, probably the best of a number in this match. This was Trott's eighth wicket of the innings, with one to fall. He took it, but as a fielder: Richardson, having tormented Giffen with some big hitting, edged him and Albert's large hands wrapped round the ball. Having bowled throughout both England innings—61.1 overs—Giffen had taken 7 for 150. But the name on everyone's lips was the newcomer from Melbourne, Albert Edwin Trott, who had taken 8 for 43 to go with his 110 runs, undefeated, in his maiden Test match. No debutant had matched those figures 100 years and over 1200 Tests later.

Trott and his captain were carried shoulder-high from the field, and soon the telegrams and prizes were pouring in, while Drewy Stoddart put down his pipe in the dining-room and answered the call to make a speech. He did it with his customary grace. His team could take their defeat. They had lost not to the weather or to bad luck. They had been beaten by a side which had played vastly better cricket. He had picked out young Trott some time earlier as a fine prospect, and he hoped he would be seen in England. And with that, he congratulated Australia on the victory, and meant every word.

Meanwhile, Albert Trott was fast being created a national hero, deified in one cartoon, and cleverly presented in a piece of rhyme. (*The Kangaroo to Mr Stoddart*):

You didn't expect it, my sonny?

Yet, truly, complain you must not;

For you wanted 'a run' for your money,

And, complying, I gave you 'a. trott'.

'Cause of Defeat'—England's cricketers allegedly on the booze during the Adelaide Test. Some critics never bothered pulling their punches.

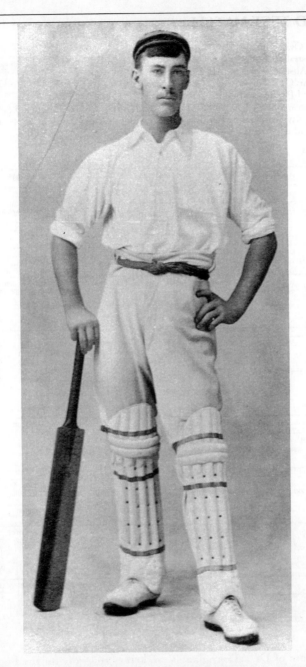

Albert Trott, who made a colossal impact in his maiden Test
and in the one which followed.

THIRD TEST MATCH

Adelaide Oval, January 11, 12, 14, 15, 1895
Toss: Australia
Debuts: Australia—J Harry, AE Trott
12th Men: CTB Turner (Aust) and LH Gay (Eng)
Umpires: J Phillips and GHG Searcy
Attendances: 5000, 12,000, 9000, 1500. Total: About 27,500 Receipts: £1154
Close of play: 1st day Eng 0-5 (MacLaren 1, Briggs 4); 2nd day Aust (2) 4-145 (Iredale 31); 3rd day Eng (2) 3-56 (Stoddart 1, Brown 2).

AUSTRALIA

First Innings / Second Innings

Batsman	First Innings		Second Innings	
W Bruce	b Richardson	11 (2)	c Brockwell b Briggs	80
GHS Trott	run out (/Peel)	48 (1)	b Peel	0
*G Giffen	c Lockwood b Brockwell	58	c Ford b Peel	24
FA Iredale	b Richardson	7	c & b Peel	140
J Darling	c Philipson b Briggs	10	c Philipson b Lockwood	3
SE Gregory	c Brown b Richardson	6	b Richardson	20
J Harry	b Richardson	2	b Richardson	6
J Worrall	run out (Richardson/Philipson)	0	c Peel b Briggs	11
†AH Jarvis	c & b Lockwood	13	c Brown b Peel	29
AE Trott	not out	38	not out	72
ST Callaway	b Richardson	41	b Richardson	11
Extras	(b2, w1, nb1)	4	(b7, lb7, nb1)	15
Total	(81.1 overs, 250 mins)	238	(115.2 overs, 330 mins)	411

Fall: 31, 69, 84, 103, 120, 124, 137, 157, 157
0, 44, 142, 145, 197, 215, 238, 283, 347

BOWLING

	O	M	R	W	w/nb		O	M	R	W	w/nb
Richardson	21.1	4	75	5	- -	(2)	31.2	8	89	3	- -
Peel	16	1	43	0	- -	(1)	34	6	96	4	- -
Brockwell	20	13	30	1	1 -	(4)	10	1	50	0	- -
Ford	8	2	19	0	- -	(6)	6	0	33	0	- -
Briggs	8	2	34	1	- -		19	3	58	2	- -
Lockwood	8	2	33	1	- 1	(3)	15	2	70	1	- 1

ENGLAND

First Innings / Second Innings

Batsman	First Innings		Second Innings	
AC MacLaren	b Callaway	25	c Iredale b AE Trott	35
J Briggs	b Callaway	12 (9)	b AE Trott	0
W Brockwell	c Harry b Callaway	12 (6)	c & b AE Trott	24
A Ward	c Bruce b Giffen	5 (2)	b AE Trott	13
*AE Stoddart	b Giffen	1 (3)	not out	34
JT Brown	not out	39 (5)	b AE Trott	2
R Peel	b Callaway	0	c & b AE Trott	0
FGJ Ford	c Worrall b Giffen	21	c GHS Trott b AE Trott	14
WH Lockwood	c Worrall b Giffen	0 (10)	c Iredale b AE Trott	1
†H Philipson	c Gregory b Giffen	7 (4)	b Giffen	1
T Richardson	c Worrall b Callaway	0	c AE Trott b Giffen	12
Extras	(b2)	2	(b5, lb2)	7
Total	(57.3 overs, 165 mins)	124	(67.1 overs, 175 mins)	143

Fall: 14, 30, 49, 50, 56, 64, 111, 111, 124
52, 52, 53, 64, 102, 102, 128, 128, 130

BOWLING

	O	M	R	W	w/nb		O	M	R	W	w/nb
AE Trott	3	1	9	0	- -	(3)	27	10	43	8	- -
Giffen	28	11	76	5	- -		33.1	12	74	2	- -
Callaway	26.3	13	37	5	- -	(1)	7	1	19	0	- -

AUSTRALIA WON BY 382 RUNS

CHAPTER ELEVEN

Upcountry

Midst the aftermath of the Adelaide Test match, one journal ran a nudge-nudge little par which may just have pointed the finger at Bobby Peel: 'The insobriety of one of the Englishmen is said to have called forth Capt. Stoddart's threat to oust the offender from the team, under the behaviour clause in their agreement, unless he steadies himself.'

Was the tour falling apart?

A welcome break of a little over a fortnight separated the third Test and the fourth, at Sydney, and the touring side's commitment was to play in Broken Hill and Dandenong.

As the miners of Broken Hill chipped away at the silver-ore faces, a major ingredient in the young country's economy, one of the English cricketers saw a piece of galena ('new chum silver'), which is worthless. Thinking it was the real thing, he asked Stoddart if he could take it. 'Stoddy' told him drily that he could fill his pockets if he wished. The captain had visited mines before.

The cricket match, over two days, was farcical. The local Eighteen lost their first five wickets without a run coming from the bat, and lost all 17 wickets for 68, Humphreys spinning more of his underhand mischief to the tune of 10 for 36 and Brockwell, the only other bowler used, taking 7 for 25. The Englishmen were not entirely at home on the matting, but MacLaren and Stoddart made fifties, and a total of 178 was enough to set up an innings win, Brockwell taking 7 for 7 this time and Philipson, given a rare bowl, spinning the ball vast distances and taking 3 for 34. Humphreys also enjoyed himself (3 for 7), and Stoddart too (4 for 18). With some daylight remaining after Broken Hill were all out for 102, the tourists gave a batting display, Ford hitting sweetly for a 78 not out which did not count. But then the match itself was anything but first-class.

They went shooting at May Bell station, the kill including lizards, wallabies, rabbits and hawks, plus a cat shot by mistake by Peel. Then a special train took them to Melbourne and thence to the Dandenong hills, where Stoddart, missed twice, carried the innings with a scintillating 81, and the local Eighteen caused mild amazement by passing the English total of 193 with 224 (Vieusseux 45, Wauchope 66, Humphreys 6 for 68, Brockwell 4 for 36). Later on the second day the tourists made 45 for 2 by the end, and during the last days of January they made their way to Sydney—where there was much rain about—for the next Test, and further sensations.

CHAPTER TWELVE

Fourth Test

Having been the first captain ever to make a declaration in a Test match (Lord's, 1893), Stoddart now became the first England skipper to put the other side in to bat upon winning the toss. And for a while the move seemed highly successful, for his bowlers took full advantage of the conditions wrought by the rain.

England were again unchanged, but Australia dropped Worrall, Harry and, despite his Adelaide runs and wickets, Callaway. In came the classy left-hander Harry Moses and the dashing little Victorian, Harry Graham, and Charlie Turner, back to full health and just the man to make full use of the rain-affected pitch.

The seas pounding the rocks around Sydney had been the roughest for 40 years, and the wild weather pattern rendered Stoddart's decision—his first of the series—horribly difficult. So he took his left-armers, Peel and Briggs, out to the middle with him, perhaps to feel again the exhilaration of that fairytale victory six weeks earlier before asking them if bowling first was the wiser course.

Peel's first ball cut a chunk out of the damp pitch and caused Harry Trott's jaw to drop. Nothing but trouble could lie ahead. After making a run, he was caught at point off Peel, and when

Stoddart (in blazer) and Giffen toss for innings at the start
of the fourth Test, at Sydney. Umpires Phillips and Bannerman are in attendance by the gate.

The stylish Sydney pavilion gazes down upon the
fourth contest of the 1894-95 series, with Australia fighting
hard to regain equal status.

Richardson launched his attack, the ball reared at Bruce's head after jagging back at him. His response was to pull and hook, and Stoddart kept adding to the leg-side field until Brockwell caught him off Peel near the fence. At 26, Peel surprised Giffen with that most unlikely of deliveries, a straight one, which bowled him, and Moses, at least as uncomfortable in these nightmare conditions as any of the others, was bowled off his pad by a full-length ball from Richardson.

The fifth wicket almost doubled the score, to 51, as Graham fearlessly, madly went down the pitch to the rampaging Richardson and hoisted him straight almost over the pickets. And as the Surrey man put even more into his shoulder action, getting the ball to buck savagely, the boyish Graham got out of danger by sinking swiftly to his knees, the crowd gasping.

When Briggs came on, he hit Graham's pads seemingly right in front, but the calm Phillips rejected the appeal. However, Gregory, maker of a double-century in the last Test here, skipped out to the same bowler, missed, and did not even both trying to get back as Philipson removed the bails: 51 for 5.

The former Australian Test captain HJH 'Tup' Scott was not the only one to have travelled a long way to see the match and to see the high-scoring Frank Iredale in particular. For them the disappointment of his first-ball dismissal now was crushing. He gently pushed a catch back to Briggs: 51 for 6, with two wickets having fallen while only a bye was added since lunch. So much for the theory that the sun was drying and easing the wicket.

Joe Darling joined Harry Graham, a good man to have at No. 8 in such a crisis. Stoddart's decision to put Australia in was vindicated already. But his fielders were to let him down.

Darling sought runs off Peel before turning his attention to Briggs, whom he hit high over the heads of the crowd into the tennis courts. 'What can you do when they just chuck one at you?' he explained later.

Graham continued to grab every run he could, but should have been caught by Brockwell at slip off Richardson when 37, a straightforward chance which tilted the innings. Darling, too, escaped when MacLaren's throw to Philipson was fumbled with the batsman short of his ground, and again when MacLaren dropped him. These English errors mattered less, for Richardson accounted for Darling at 31, though not in a way that pleased him. Overstretching himself in his attempt to bowl a yorker, he flung down a beamer, and Darling's frantic stab at it merely deflected the ball into his stumps: 119 for 7, the stand worth 68 in only 40 minutes.

In came the hero of Adelaide, Albert Trott, only to take a fast one from Richardson that laid him out for a minute or two, a number of Englishmen gathering round solicitously, some rubbing the point of impact. When the young Victorian eventually resumed, he looked very determined.

Graham had raced to a 65-minute half-century and then had another close shave, mishitting Briggs high into the sky. The bowler failed to hold the catch as it plummeted earthwards, and one of the earliest instances of 'sledging' was then recorded by *The Australasian*: 'Johnny was either annoyed with himself or with the batsman's luck, and delivered a short lecturette on the total ignorance of Australians of the art of batting, but a reminder from the tactful Stoddart sent him to his bowling again.'

When Ford was tried, Graham twice beautifully square-drove him to the fence, and Trott pulled him to the same joyous spectators. By tea they had lifted the total to 192 for 7, Graham 87, Trott 40, and England revealing a touch of desperation, Brockwell having just spilled a caught-and-bowled from Graham.

Local delight contrasted with the earlier depression when Australia were more than half out for 51. Now, a youngster leaned over the pickets and bellowed out a strange challenge to any of the Englishmen of £100 to nothing that Harry Graham would make more off his own bat than their whole team.

It hardly helped England that they were carrying a passenger in Bill Lockwood, who had got into further trouble, this time not of his own doing, when a soda-water bottle held by Peel had exploded, cutting Lockwood's left hand. It was hoped that the wound would heal as the match progressed, but it worsened, and a doctor had to open it up again. His bowling was limited to the final phase, and he was not fit to bat when the time came.

Graham and Trott took Australia to 200, prompting happy strangers in the crowd to shake hands with each other, and as the reformed pitch drew the sting of the bowling, Richardson actually had to protect the straight boundaries either side. The duel had been won, and memorable it had been.

Graham reached his century with a hit to the square-leg fence off Peel, his 14th four, in only 140 minutes, bringing him immortality as the only batsman—in the first 100 years and more of England v Australia Test cricket—to score a century in his first Test innings in both countries. For those who saw either or both performances, it was far more than a statistical achievement. What thrilled was the manner of the making of those runs.

He was out soon after, charging at Briggs and being stumped by a long way. The prayed-for breakthrough, after all those gallant hits and scrambled singles, had come. Eight runs later, Jarvis was caught behind, giving Johnny Briggs his 100th Test wicket. The fun-loving epileptic was the first bowler to reach this mark, but it was a far less statistics-conscious age.

All that could be said by England for the 10th-wicket stand which followed was that at least it was not as large as the two in Adelaide (81 and 64). But the 45 put on by Trott, who was loving Test cricket, and Turner, who was one of the best No. 11s ever to bat for Australia, did little to restore sinking English spirits. Would young Trott get his hundred this time? Turner tried hard to see him to it, but himself was caught at mid-off off Lockwood. Australia had hauled themselves up to 284, and AE Trott's unbeaten 85 (105 minutes) gave him 195 runs now in Test cricket without dismissal. This time he had added more cuts and leg placements to his basic firm-footed driving, and unless an outstretched MacLaren hand running round the boundary counted as a miss, the innings was chanceless.

England had to survive 10 minutes that evening against Harry Trott's legspin and Turner's offcutters. MacLaren, by little more than an inch, was stumped off Trott almost immediately. There were screeches when Briggs seemed to be out too, but he was merely teasing, the 'catch' having come off his body. Eleven for one wicket; England had everything to pray for; the 8000-odd wended their way happily home.

SECOND DAY

It rained and rained, and people sat around mournfully, though the Englishmen seemed content that the downpour was heavy enough to spare them from having to slither about out there against Turner, Giffen and company. Play was called off around 4 pm, and the hardy 4000 were given passout tickets for Monday.

THIRD DAY

Sunday was fine, and had there been play England might have had reasonable conditions at their disposal. But Monday brought a return to rain, borne in on a stiff southwesterly, and when play was possible, batting hardly was.

Seventeen English wickets fell that day. It would almost certainly have been 19 had Lockwood been fit to bat. Around 16,000 people saw the visitors committed to nothing short of torture as they went to the wicket and saw all normal understanding of bat-versus-ball obliterated by the soft pitch. Giffen took eight wickets, Turner seven, and Harry Trott added two to his overnight one. His brother did not even get on, just when his best Test figures of 8 for 43 less than three weeks before might have been shattered.

Stoddart made no secret of his expectations. England, he said, would be bowled out twice that day on that mudheap. He was right, with over an hour to spare.

Everyone expected Giffen to start with Albert Trott, but it was Trott snr who spun his legbreaks, with Turner at the other end, often beating the bat but kicking the ball well over the bails. It was as if the ball was being jerked on the end of a piece of string.

Ward went first, caught low down by Turner the bowler, and after much patting of the pitch and nimble attempts to counter the ball, Briggs swung, missed and was bowled by Harry Trott, who next spun one out of Stoddart's reach, but not wicketkeeper Jarvis's. The stumping of the captain, who had more marks on his shirt-

front than on his bat, made it 31 for 4. Turner had three short
legs for Brockwell, and when he switched to around the wicket, the
batsman played firmly to midwicket, only to see Darling's hand
thrust up for the catch: 40 for 5.

The fair-minded romantics now felt that justice would be done
if the pitch eased, for Australia's early agony had been dispelled by
better batting conditions, of which Graham, Darling and Albert
Trott had taken massive advantage. Such was not England's fate.
The ball went on leaping impossibly, no less when Giffen gave
himself a bowl as Ford came in. He licked his fingertips, ran in
easily, and spun one across the left-hander, who played to leg but
was caught at point.

The only Australian error of the day came when Giffen missed
a return catch from Brown. Peel was smartly stumped by Jarvis for
his third successive Test duck, and at lunch England, half-drowned,
were 59 for 7, Brown 20, Philipson 0.

Philipson resumed with a four off Giffen, who then had him
caught at midwicket and held a low left-handed return catch in his
followthrough to get Richardson and close the innings for 65. The
pitch was rolled and rendered a little less spiteful, and England
went in again. This time, Turner and Giffen completed the job.

Brown opened with Ward and was bowled fourth ball, yorked
as he aimed a big drive at Giffen. Stoddart desperately lofted Turner
towards the ladies' stand and was caught without scoring, and when
Bruce stuck up a hand to arrest a crisp hit by MacLaren, England
were 5 for three wickets, all those dismissed being scoreless.

Stoddart's spirits were low. 'It's the worst wicket I've ever seen,'
he was heard to say, 'absolutely the worst; and not only is it the
worst I've seen,' he added, in case anyone should have been left in
any doubt, 'but it's miles the worst!'

With Philipson, Ford and Major Wardill he had driven to
Coogee on the rest day, to the Australians' camp, but he must now
have felt little like fraternising.

Ward realised that his usual caution would be misplaced, so he
hit out–and Darling ran in, steadied himself and held the catch:
12 for 4. Peel was then stumped again, getting his second 'pair'

running in some style: 14 for 5. Ford and Brockwell found the boundary, but it was merely to reduce the degree of humiliation. Life had to be short. Brockwell got hold of a ball from Turner, but Bruce held the catch to give CTB Turner his 100th Test wicket, though very little fuss was made about it.

Bruce now fielded in close as Giffen bowled to Briggs, and a mighty swipe was parried by the Victorian left-hander, the catch gently held on the rebound: 47 for 7. Next, Ford hit Giffen straight back only to see Darling pocket another neat catch. With one wicket to fall—Lockwood again out of action, his arm in a sling—a macabre day's cricket neared its close with the square-leg umpire taking a whack on the side of the head from Richardson's leg-side heave during a ninth-wicket stand of 20 which was the highest in either England innings. It was a matter of euthanasia when Philipson drove back to Turner and the final score was 72, giving Australia victory by an innings and 147 runs, their heaviest to date. Turner gave the ball to Giffen, who presented it to a lady in the reserve.

The Australians were greeted warmly in the pavilion, and the *Sydney Morning Herald* shrewdly observed that 'they were no longer Victorians or South Australians or New South Welshmen, they were all Australians, and all jolly good fellows.'

Throughout the carnage, Jarvis had coped well enough to allow only 12 byes and to complete four stumpings as the ball hopped and buzzed and skidded. It was remarked that England's bowling lacked variety in that it was either fast right-arm or slow left-arm. Turner and Giffen, more potently, brought the ball back at the batsman.

Australia's bowlers had unquestionably done all that was expected of them as the series was levelled. But victory would not necessarily have been theirs had not Harry Graham carved out his wonderful century. 'Game as a pebble', he was said to have found everything in Sydney agreeable except the passionfruit. Among the gifts heaped upon him were four pipes, three hats, a box of cigars, orders for three suits, and a new bat.

Ecstatic he may have been, but the Englishmen were slightly wary of the large crowd of spectators who still waited by the exit

Victoria's 'little dasher' Harry Graham, who hit a stirring
hundred at Sydney in his first home Test and helped
Australia level the series.

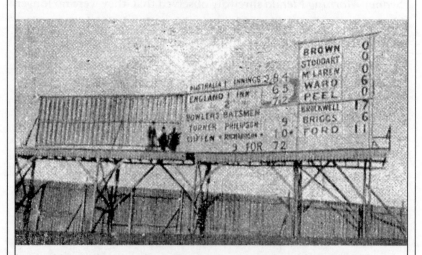

The tables turned: after Turner and Giffen had wrought
havoc, England have been thrashed in the fourth Test, revers-
ing the amazing outcome of the opening Test of the series at
the SCG.

long after play had ended. Billy Brockwell, top-scorer in the final innings with a mere 17, and whose home was The Oval, eyed the gathering with a certain suspicion, and wrote: 'It is a demonstrative, ribald crowd that, especially the boy section of it, has so much to say in a way that is personal that even a big man like Lyons won't face it alone.'

And a sense of humour was also called for in the face of some of the mail received. Drewy Stoddart received a letter the next day, in a neat hand, which read: 'One Australian and two Yorkshire lassies wish to express their deepest sympathy with Messrs Stoddart & Co at their misfortune in only making five duck eggs, & send the enclosed to make the half dozen. Having staked their "little all" on the event & *lost*, they cannot afford to have it gilded, but trust that after the Melbourne event *you* will be able to put it in a golden case.'

In their anguish, the girls got one simple thing wrong: there were not five English ducks in their sad innings of 65 and 72. There were six.

The evils of the Sydney pitch are examined at close quarters minutes after the fourth Test had ended.

FOURTH TEST MATCH

Sydney Cricket Ground, February 1, 2 (no play), 4, 1895
Toss: England
Debuts: None
12th Men: CE McLeod (Aust) and LH Gay (Eng)
Umpires: C Bannerman and J Phillips
Attendances: 8277, no play (4158), 15,953. Total: 24,230 (excluding second day)
    Receipts: £1178
Close of play: 1st day Eng 1-11 (Ward 5, Briggs 4); 2nd day no play.

AUSTRALIA
First Innings

GHS Trott	c Brown b Peel	1
W Bruce	c Brockwell b Peel	15
*G Giffen	b Peel	8
H Moses	b Richardson	1
H Graham	st Philipson b Briggs	105
SE Gregory	st Philipson b Briggs	5
FA Iredale	c & b Briggs	0
J Darling	b Richardson	31
AE Trott	not out	85
†AH Jarvis	c Philipson b Briggs	5
CTB Turner	c Richardson b Lockwood	22
Extras	(b3, lb1, w1, nb1)	6
Total	(83.5 overs, 245 mins)	284

Fall: 2, 20, 26, 26, 51, 51, 119, 231, 239

BOWLING	O	M	R	W	w/nb
Peel	24	5	74	3	- -
Richardson	22	5	78	2	- -
Briggs	22	4	65	4	1 -
Brockwell	5	1	25	0	- -
Ford	2	0	14	0	- -
Lockwood	8.5	3	22	1	- 1

ENGLAND
First Innings   *Second Innings*

AC MacLaren	st Jarvis b GHS Trott	1	(4)	c Bruce b Giffen	0
A Ward	c & b Turner	7		c Darling b Giffen	6
J Briggs	b GHS Trott	11	(8)	c Bruce b Giffen	6
*AE Stoddart	st Jarvis b GHS Trott	7	(3)	c Iredale b Turner	0
JT Brown	not out	20	(1)	b Giffen	0
W Brockwell	c Darling b Turner	1	(5)	c Bruce b Turner	17
FGJ Ford	c GHS Trott b Giffen	0		c Darling b Giffen	11
R Peel	st Jarvis b Turner	0	(6)	st Jarvis b Turner	0
†H Philipson	c Graham b Giffen	4		c & b Turner	9
T Richardson	c & b Giffen	2		not out	10
WH Lockwood	absent hurt	-		absent hurt	-
Extras	(b7, lb3, nb2)	12		(b5, lb7, nb1)	13
Total	(38.5 overs, 115 mins)	65		(29.1 overs, 94 mins)	72

Fall: 2, 20, 24, 31, 40, 43, 56, 63, 65
0, 5, 5, 12, 14, 29, 47, 52, 72

BOWLING	O	M	R	W	w/nb		O	M	R	W	w/nb
GHS Trott	14	5	21	3	- -						
Turner	19	10	18	3	- 2		14.1	6	33	4	- 1
Giffen	5.5	1	14	3	- -	(1)	15	7	26	5	- -

AUSTRALIA WON BY AN INNINGS AND 147 RUNS

CHAPTER THIRTEEN

Drawing Breath

There was all but a month between the fourth and fifth Tests, and there were but three match commitments for Stoddart's team in that time while the nation chattered tensely in anticipation of the deciding Test match to come in Melbourne.

The Englishmen travelled back up to New England to play again at Armidale, where they had given less than due attention to their job in December, having been bowled out for 67 before recovering in the second innings. Now, Brockwell, Brown, Peel and Ward were all out to left-arm medium-pacer Cooper with only 20 on the board. Stoddart's 88 brought some masterly batting and respectability to the event, though he was dropped twice. The aim now was to restore confidence after the two Test losses. He also left behind him in Sydney rumours linking him with a North Shore girl and suggesting he was about to settle in the metropolis.

MacLaren came in near the tail and made 41, and on the second day the New England XXII fell short of England's 187 by 76 runs, Peel taking 11 for 45 (nine of them bowled). The English XI went in again and had a hit, though it remained difficult to penetrate a field populated by 18 fielders. They finished with 112 for 7, made some complimentary remarks about the New England

Some of the English cricketers and their hosts return from a shoot in the bush. Some were good shots and some emphatically were not.

bowling, and left the townsfolk well pleased with their visit.

The team then moved on to Brisbane, to the Exhibition Ground again, where they played a Combined XI, Queensland players boosted by some of their recent New South Wales opposition, a strong side which included Coningham, Iredale, Gregory, Turner and Callaway from the recent Tests and Percy McDonnell, the former Australian captain and big hitter. Also playing was Tom McKibbin, who had taken 5 for 19 and 9 for 68 for NSW a few days earlier as they beat Queensland. He bowled offcutters and was clearly a threat to Turner for a place in the final Test.

The weather remained mixed, but the Englishmen batted and were overcoming an awkward start of 43 for 3, Stoddart and MacLaren in control, when Charlie Bannerman no-balled Coningham, who blew his top. He ran in again and, before reaching the umpire, let fly a throw at Stoddart, who was shocked by it and demanded an apology to himself and Bannerman. It was some time before Coningham muttered an apology, and his next delivery bowled the England captain, who was visibly upset. He would not have expected behaviour such as this even on the rugby field.

Stoddart's 40 was top score, but Peel was delighted with his 30 after all those Test ducks, and the total of 192 seemed reasonable when rain gingered up the pitch on the second day. Richardson (5 for 42) was fast and dangerous, and Briggs diddled out four in the second half for 15: 107 all out, the rain/hot sun combination proving a huge influence yet again.

Richardson had put two batsmen, Sammy Jones and the wicket-keeper Bradley, out of the match with blows respectively to knee and hand, and Iredale was the second substitute wicketkeeper, gratifyingly for MacLaren, whom he dropped on 99. MacLaren, the only batsman to pass 50 in the match, scored an impressive two-hour century, and Ward 47, in a second innings of 279 which left Combined NSW & Queensland—two men short—needing 365 for victory. Richardson and Briggs dispatched them for 86. Iredale extended his successful run against English bowling with an unbeaten 33 to go with his 37 not out, but Syd Gregory could manage no more than 15 and 16, and Callaway bagged a 'pair'. McKibbin, though, increased his chances of selection for the final Test match by taking 5 for 98, moving the ball either way. Turner will have been an anxious man.

The tourists now moved down to Newcastle for a match against an Eighteen drawn from clubs in Newcastle, Maitland, Singleton and Muswellbrook. It was a great relief to escape the sapping heat and humidity of Brisbane.

The locals made 189 (Lockwood 6 for 51) and Ward and Brockwell had 67 up by the close. Rain then flooded the ground, and when they were able to get going again on the second day, the first-wicket stand was extended to 146, the highest by England on their tour. As the sun did its work, batting became more difficult, though Stoddart did belt one ball right out of the neat little ground, to go with the wicket he had taken with his first ball.

He would not let Lockwood bat, fearing a blow would set his injured hand back, so nine out was all out, for 241, 52 ahead. The Northern District XVIII were 87 for 5 by the end, and everyone was happy.

Stoddart and his band broke their journey to Melbourne with a stop in Sydney, watching some of the NSW v South Australia match, and yet more runs by Iredale (91) and Gregory (66) and more bowling by the inexhaustible Giffen.

During the tea interval, in the presence of the Sheffield Shield teams, the Englishmen were toasted by the NSW Premier GH Reid, who was also president of the NSWCA. The game had been greatly forwarded by the visit of Mr Stoddart and his team, he said, and the good feeling between the old country and the colonies had never been more in evidence. They did not think less of the Englishmen because the Australians had got level with them. He called for three cheers for the tourists, and Stoddart made a quiet, sincere response.

Then off they went to Melbourne for the climax of the campaign. Steamers and trains were converging on the city for the 'great Test match', Kangaroo v Lion, the greatest show on earth, with Australia favourites now they had won twice by colossal margins and had the brilliant youngsters Harry Graham and Albert Trott to fight alongside George Giffen and the older brigade. Even at the net practices, over 1000 eager fans gathered to watch. Major Wardill was supervising all kinds of extra seating and covering arrangements at the MCG, and it was remarked that the city was not only suffering more traffic congestion than usual but its streets were full of strangers. They came from interstate and from bush towns. Men planned absences from their offices and boys worked on schemes to make the money for admission to the cricket.

The universal prayer was that this time there should be no sticky wicket to disadvantage one of the teams—unless perhaps it was to the favour of one's own!

But rain or shine, for all who were partial to cricket, there was only one place to be, the Melbourne Cricket Ground—while over in England, the Thames was frozen over and people were skating on the pond near Stoddart's Hampstead home.

And gentlemen in England now abed
Shall think themselves accurs'd they were not here.

CHAPTER FOURTEEN

Fifth Test

Friday, March 1, 1895. Trams and horsedrawn cabs carry their eager human cargo to the MCG. Pedestrians tread with undisguised purpose through the parks towards the centre of activity. All is buzz and chatter as finally the two captains emerge, arm in arm with Major Ben Wardill, Melbourne Cricket Club secretary and tour organiser. Two-all, and this is the decider.

'I knew that when Stoddart and I went into the ring to toss and arrange preliminaries,' Giffen was to write, 'he was as white as a sheet, and I have been told that the pallor of my own countenance matched his.'

The tension was getting to everybody, even Wardill, who grew impatient with the delay as Stoddart and Giffen discussed such matters as the rolling and mowing of the pitch: 'For Heaven's sake, toss and get it over with!'

'Keep cool, Major,' soothed the England captain, as Giffen, hand shaking, spun the coin given to him by a friend. 'Heads,' called Stoddart. It came to rest tails up. Cheers went up as word spread, but Stoddart's look of despair seemed to be saying 'It's all over'. Giffen again decided to keep the coin.

While England again remained unchanged in line-up, Australia

Top left: Archie MacLaren warms up at Melbourne, where he made the first of his five centuries against Australia, an invaluable 120.

Opposite: England, having lost the previous two Tests, practise hard in the hope of recapturing some of the earlier momentum for the all-or-nothing final Test.

Above: Australia, fifth Test, Melbourne, 1894-95. *Standing:* J Darling, JJ Lyons, W Bruce, H Graham, GHS Trott, FA Iredale; *seated:* AE Trott, G Giffen (captain), SE Gregory; *in front:* AH Jarvis, TR McKibbin.

omitted Moses and Turner, whose angry reaction was 'I'll never play cricket again!'

'It's no use talking like that, Charlie,' said Jack Lyons, who was back in the side following an attacking century against Victoria. 'You'll have to go to England if we go next year.' But the Terror had played his last Test. McKibbin's 14 wickets against South Australia at Sydney had made his selection irresistible.

There had been talk of adopting national colours of olive and gold by the Australians, but for the time being they wore the dark blue of Melbourne, and with Billy Bruce having hurried across from his duties at North Melbourne police court, he and Harry Trott steadied their nerves and strode out after the England fielders. Trott felt in touch, having made 152 in 3 1/4 hours on this ground against South Australia a fortnight earlier.

Richardson and Peel opened the bowling for England.

Bruce, without having had a warm-up, soon settled, and revealed his mannerism of putting his left hand in his pocket as a back-cut sent the ball to the third-man boundary. Then an explosive delivery from Richardson split his bat in two, and he was caught off his replacement blade by MacLaren at the second attempt after cutting at Peel, whose length had settled: 40 for 1.

Giffen shed his multi-coloured blazer and walked to the middle, fixing on his gloves. Trott had already been missed by Ford at slip at 9 off Peel, brushing the memory aside with a robust drive for four that had one enthusiast crying out, music-hall fashion, 'Good boy, 'Arry!' And Giffen was soon at ease, driving hard across Tom McCutcheon's smooth outfield.

But there was a sense of deadly earnest about proceedings. Stoddart was seen as 'not only a tactician but a mathematician, for he seemed to make 11 men go into 15 places and have one over to back up'. The Englishmen fielded like tigers, and when Lockwood came on to bowl he made his first real impression on the series. Australia were well satisfied to go to lunch at 76 for the loss of only Bruce.

In a subdued light and with the ground now filling up, the decisive match continued, the 100 being greeted noisily. But then

Trott tried to hit to leg against Briggs and was bowled. 'Played it on, Harry?' someone called from the members' area. 'No,' said Trott obligingly, 'clean bowled.'

The prolific Iredale replaced him, slightly unwell but cool under his new white quilted hat, his bat black at the rear from constant patting down of wet divot-marks on pitches around Australia.

Runs were very hard to find. England's bowling and fielding were at their best, and a classic test of wills was taking place, only 25 runs coming in three-quarters of an hour before Richardson's fast breakback proved too much for Iredale: 126 for 3.

Gregory, the pint-size 24-year-old, made his way to the crease, the fifth of eight frontline batsmen in the side, and soon took a four to leg off Richardson.

Giffen was patient, taking a rare boundary which prompted a lad to yell out, just as the cheering subsided, 'That's an all-righter, ain't it!' A century seemed on the cards. He passed 50. Then Peel bowled a full-toss and the Australian captain, in his eagerness to make it count, brought it into his stumps. This was Australia's lowest ebb: 142 for 4. But Gregory and Darling were to double the score and put their side notionally ahead.

Darling was chancy at first, especially in lifting his off-drives, but he gradually looked more comfortable, while 'Tich' Gregory went for his shots, including the nimble-footed pull. Richardson seemed to be bowling even faster later in the day, striving for the breakthrough which would set up Ashes victory, and Briggs was anything but his normal teasing self, pushing the ball through with less flight—which may just have been a mistake.

Ford ought to have caught Gregory when he was 19, and the batsman gratefully took 13 off a Brockwell over; Darling too was let off, when 46, Philipson putting him down off Lockwood. By the end, Australia were 282 for 4, Gregory, up on tiptoes time and again to steer the ball away for runs, now 70 in 130 minutes, Darling, who should have been run out by Ward—his one mistake in a grand afternoon's fielding—on 72 in just under two hours. The great contest everybody craved was taking shape.

SECOND DAY

The Saturday brought warm sun which 'made the blood tingle nicely in the veins and the money jingle nicely in the till boxes. There never was such a day.' Nor such an MCG crowd, for it eventually numbered close to 30,000, with much discomfort having to be endured in the shoulder-to-shoulder crush. People were hanging onto balustrades and straining for a view, the lucky ones having been there early, rushing the front seats when the turnstiles were opened at 10.30, an hour and a half before the start of play. It would have been even worse had there not been a race meeting at Flemington that afternoon.

A double breakthrough came immediately. With two runs added, Darling nicked Peel to slip, where Ford calmly held the catch one-handed. So much for Darling's father's incentive of a 25-guinea gold watch if he made a century—though Mr Darling relented and gave it to Joe anyway. Two more runs later, Gregory got a touch to one of Richardson's rockets, and Philipson, the wicketkeeper, held it: 286 for 6.

Lyons and Graham made an unusually formidable seventh-wicket pair, both Test century-makers, both in form, both capable of gracing a top-order position. England had to separate them quickly.

Tom Richardson proved reliable again. Graham had played a sweet leg-glance, but now the Surrey man delivered what the locals referred to as a 'clinker' of a ball, finding the edge as little Graham went up on his toes, only to have his stumps smashed by a huge breakback. Honest Tom was getting some reward at last.

Albert Trott came in with every appearance of nonchalance, which 195 Test runs without dismissal could easily breed.

The 300 was up by now, and Trott presented a familiar menace to England—until, at 10, he lifted one to Lockwood at cover off Peel, and departed with a Test average at last (205). It was suggested that the young man may have learned this deviant shot from having spent so much time of late coaching the lady cricketers.

In came the broad figure of Jarvis, and with his tendency to step forward at the same time as he moved his right leg back towards the stumps, he smeared an off-side delivery round to the leg boundary, and gave his fellow South Australian, Lyons, a big knowing wink. Lyons, in turn, did Australia a favour by twice hitting Richardson for four, only MacLaren's speed on the boundary stopping a third, the Surrey man then being given a spell. His county team-mate Lockwood came on, and soon Lyons (55) was gone, caught behind by Philipson. But McKibbin, in his first Test, stayed with Jarvis to lunch, when Australia were 385 for 9, and hoping for just a few more.

They pushed the total up to 414 before McKibbin, averaging 70 in his last three innings for his club, and now using Blackham's bat, was lured to destruction by Briggs for 23 out of a last-wicket stand of 47 which reflected an almost routine source of frustration for England in this series.

The mammoth crowd were well pleased, with one of their number, Tom Horan ('Felix' the journalist), who could find room only on the players' balcony, enthusing about the visiting players again: 'Today there is no regret, save that we are so soon to see the last of the gallant band who are fighting so hard for England, home, and beauty. I like them so well that I wish they could stay with us for ever. They are the most popular team that ever came to Australia, and as for their captain, why the reception he gets whenever he comes out to bat makes me feel proud of my countrymen.'

Stoddart decided to send Brockwell in with Ward to open, but Brockwell's huge opening stands for Surrey with Bobby Abel were several years in the future, and the experiment failed here at Melbourne, Harry Trott bringing him forward and having him stumped for 5 with his first ball. Brockwell was heard to remark later: 'Well, I've tried everything—going in late, playing steadily, hitting hard, but somehow I can't get going.' Most batsmen know the feeling.

The England captain was given a reception of such warmth that he might easily have been one of their own. He and Ward were restrained. Neither was ever likely to play in a more important match or before such a large crowd. All they had fought for over the past three months was at stake. Australia's best bowler, Turner, was not playing, but Giffen, the Trotts and new boy McKibbin were, and if ever that modern word 'pressure' were applicable to play in the Naughty Nineties it was now.

Often Stoddart made as if to go for runs, only to slacken the wrists and back down. He moved into the twenties, then late-cut Giffen to the iron railings for his first boundary. Others followed, including a square-leg hit off his opposite number which caused Giffen to waver. McKibbin, pride of Bathurst, came on, moving the ball either way, though erratic in length, and Stoddart glanced him for runs. Albert Trott was also tried, and Albert Ward unleashed some commanding drives through the covers, celebrating a let-off to Harry Trott at point in McKibbin's first over. When Stoddart played a maiden out with studious care, he smiled gently as he picked up the strains from the outer of 'Well played, Bannerman!' He had done his share of fielding out to the little Australian stonewaller.

Stoddart reached 50 and was in line for a Melbourne century to go with the one in the second Test. But at 68 Harry Trott spun one past him and Jarvis completed the stumping, the batsman shaking his head at Phillips' confirmation from square leg not in dissent but annoyance that he should have fallen into the same trap in successive Tests. One report said the ball turned 'abruptly to leg', so if it was not a variation offbreak it must have been an early googly or wrong'un, nine years before the trick ball was recognised following Bosanquet's regular and successful exploitation of it. Whatever it was, it produced a key breakthrough to leave England 110 for 2—soon to be made worse as McKibbin broke through Ward, whose 32 had taken almost two hours: 112 for 3.

MacLaren, who had made only 100 runs at 16 in the series so far, joined Brown, and both played confidently, Brown strong on the cut, MacLaren making runs stylishly on the leg side, sometimes employing the 'Harrow leg glide', though once almost sweeping round and hitting his wicket.

Jack Brown suddenly got out. Albert Trott flung down a breakback on a length, and the Yorkshireman was bowled for 30, leaving

England 166 for 4, and causing the first fears among the locals that there might be another compulsory follow-on, strong England second innings and Australian collapse after either rain or natural deterioration of the pitch. It was these irrationalities which eventually led to the amendment in 1900 whereby the follow-on was optional for the team in control.

There were no further casualties that day as MacLaren moved to 40 and Peel to 18, relieved to have put a stop to the series of four Test ducks. The talk that Saturday night was of how poorly Giffen had bowled—blows on his right hand from Lockwood and Richardson while batting on the first day having left the bowling hand sore—and of MacLaren's enchanting and convincing strokes, reminders of that double-century made here against Victoria when the Englishmen were fresh from their outward voyage.

THIRD DAY

The Sunday of rest brought no spoiling rain, and Monday also broke fine. It was a business day, but it was still estimated that the attendance, including members, would have touched 20,000. They had another engrossing day's cricket. The *Argus* man noted that from the sea of colour all round the perimeter, 'two spots stood out vividly—a scarlet sunshade on the other side of the ground, a bright yellow one in the reserve. They caught the eye so quickly that had either been in the line of the wickets, England or the parasols must have collapsed'.

England did not collapse. Against Albert Trott and McKibbin, Peel and MacLaren picked up runs from the start, a four-wides being a welcome present from Trott. Giffen came on, but it made little difference. Fifty runs came in 45 minutes.

Peel then had some rich fortune. Lofting Giffen, he saw the reliable Iredale toss away his hat, chase, lunge, and miss the catch: Peel had his fifty. The bowler, still troubled by his damaged hand, then missed a return catch from MacLaren when he was 69. It may have been MacLaren who went down to the railings for a quick sip, prompting a female spectator to offer him a whiff of her smelling-salts. By then, Johnny Briggs, who had coached MacLaren ever since he

Midway through the absorbing final Test, Harry Trott is seen spinning one down to Albert Ward before a packed MCG.

The longer the 1894-95 Test series went on the greater became the public's hunger for news. Here, cricket-lovers in Melbourne spill over into the roadway as they try to catch a glimpse of the progress board outside the offices of the *Argus* and *Australasian.*

first appeared for Lancashire, was aglow with pride. At last the young man with the imperious manner was proving his worth in a Test match.

The strong wind blew thistledown from the plains outside across the outfield as thinkers in the audience wondered why Harry Trott's legbreaks weren't tried. They did not know that Giffen believed they were impotent against left-hand batting, and Peel looked in good fettle. MacLaren was clamped by three close leg-side fielders when Giffen bowled, but the pair made it safely to lunch at 295 for 4, the absence of a wicket in that session causing the crowd to modulate its reception to MacLaren (78) and Peel (66) and to show a certain impatience with the Australians, who now looked less like a collective, with McKibbin (wearing light blue) and Albert Trott (South Australian black-and-yellow sash) departing from the Melbourne dark blue, Syd Gregory going even further with the colours presented him by an English club on the 1893 tour.

Some onlookers were completely baffled by Giffen when he came out wearing a large grey felt hat which gave him the appearance of having no neck. Who was the substitute? they enquired.

The total was raised to 328, the stand worth 162, before Peel was caught at mid-off off Giffen for 73, and MacLaren affectionately escorted him back and returned to the middle with Lockwood. He lasted only a short time before propping a catch to silly mid-on, and wickets fell with regularity thereafter, the seventh, eighth and ninth while only two runs were made.

MacLaren was tired. He went down on one knee and sometimes came close to reclining full-length between overs. Ford crashed the ball back at Harry Trott, who failed to hold the catch and took the ball ruefully on the ear, the bowler also suffering when Giffen put Ford down at slip.

By now, Archie MacLaren, the lordly young Lancastrian, had his hundred, reached with an on-driven boundary off Albert Trott after 175 minutes at the crease. At 114 he was reprieved by Giffen from a caught-and-bowled, but at the same score as he lost Ford, 364, he spun into a swivelling hook at Harry Trott and accidentally nudged his stumps. His 120 had lasted 220 minutes, with 12 memorable fours.

Two runs later, Harry Trott fell and held a one-handed catch at silly mid-on to administer Briggs a duck, but Philipson and Richardson conjured up 19 for the last wicket, taking England to 385, only 29 behind Australia, before Harry Trott had Richardson lbw, only the third leg-before of the entire series (there were two important ones still to come) in an age when the ball had to pitch between wicket and wicket.

Under an overcast sky, with a thunderstorm threatening, Australia sought to build on their slender lead. Harry Trott was watchful, as was Billy Bruce, who was supposed to be leading the scoring, and after a slow-scoring start, Giffen ran out with a replacement bat for Bruce which was really a pretext for imparting a plea to him to get on with it. The people of Melbourne felt rather resentful when Bruce hit a catch back to Peel two balls later.

Trott and Giffen survived, little else, until the end of play, allowing Lockwood to bowl eight overs for a cost of only two runs, with Peel almost as economical. The hot day closed with Australia 69 for 1, 98 ahead.

FOURTH DAY

The weather changed, though not to rain. A roaring wind carried red dust over everything. 'Seen from a distance,' wrote the reluctant *Argus* reporter, 'the MCG looked anything but a picnic spot. One looked down onto a valley of dust, with just the roof of the pavilion and the tops of the elm trees peeping through.'

As spectators chased their hats, Harry Trott edged a fast four off Lockwood. The awning on the ladies' reserve was torn away by the gale, and the rattling scoreboard had to be roped down. Charlie Turner's girlfriend's parasol was blown inside-out, and poor little Briggs had an attack of stringhalt and Stoddart placed his shivering player at point until the spasm had passed. It was small surprise that Trott soon missed one from Peel which was on target, giving rise to an early reference to 'one which came with the bowler's arm'.

Trott had made 42, as in the first innings, and Australia were 75 for 2.

Iredale joined Giffen, Australia's most secure pair, and 50 more runs came. They had less patience with the Australian captain than his home crowd at Adelaide Oval, and as the tedium mounted, a plaintive cry came from the ring: 'George Giffen, how much longer are you going to play this game?' The canny batsman's response was a lovely off-drive for four off Lockwood.

The wind swung round, so Peel changed ends. So dour was the batting that Stoddart was able to close the field in, denying singles. And just before lunch, Iredale played Richardson onto his boot and thence into the wicket, giving the bowler the luck he had been missing: 125 for 3, 154 ahead.

By force of character, Giffen was endeavouring to win this inexpressibly important match off his own bat. It was his nature. He would bowl until every opponent was out, and he would bat, if he could, until enough runs had been made. It took an equally eager Richardson to stop him. The ball burst through, via the bat, into his stumps: 148 for 4. It was Giffen's second half-century of the match, to go with his four wickets in 45 overs, but his departure permitted the English cricketers to believe once again that they could win this one. (Giffen's personal triumph stemmed from having been dismissed just this once by Richardson in this series, having fallen to him just on a dozen times during the 1893 tour.)

It was another of Richardson's great bowling spells, when his strength and purpose marked him as the best in the world. His captain never had need to pamper him. He would offer to bowl all day, and gave the batsmen no let-up, pounding the ball in on a difficult length, with wrist and finger working it so that it deviated malevolently from outside off stump and often went inside the insecure bat, causing the wicketkeeper to hurl himself to the left. It was such a breakback which now bowled Gregory for 30, and when Briggs spun one through Lyons, Australia were 200 for 6, some way from security.

Newspapers blew across the ground, and when one lodged in one of the trees, a shortsighted man asked, 'What's that white in the tree?' 'The ghost of the man who planted it,' said his neighbour, 'come back to see Richardson bowl.'

Australia's hope now was that depth of batting would see them through. Darling (28) and Graham (10) were together at tea, the total 218 for 6, the youthful Graham having lifted spirits by the very way he had walked in to bat, swinging his bat merrily. Richardson had quickly crashed a ball into his thigh, but the 'Little Dasher' then swung him away for four.

After the interval, though, the red-hot Richardson hit him on the pad as he swung wildly, and the umpire's finger was raised, casting a mournful silence over much of the gathering. It was even worse two balls later when Richardson, the strong wind behind him, took his fifth wicket by bowling Albert Trott, who had taken guard and barely observed the field around him. In that fatal flash his freak average dropped to 102.50, there to stay forever, highest still in Ashes Tests 100 years later.

This was grim for Australia: two wickets remaining, 248 ahead. Darling and Jarvis had a mid-pitch mix-up, but Philipson's frenzied throw was to the wrong end and made the crowd scream as two overthrows were scrambled. Jarvis looked secure, even against Richardson, and Darling's big hit against Briggs persuaded Stoddart that Peel should be brought back. Left-hander Darling went to 50 with two fours off Richardson, and the initiative was easing back to Australia—until Darling jumped out at Peel and yorked himself: 248 for 9. McKibbin made a precious 13 of 19 added for the final wicket, and then he too fell to Richardson, caught behind, giving the fast bowler 6 for 104, and nine wickets in the match, in which he had bowled 87.2 overs. Peel had wheeled down 94 overs, taking 7 for 203, and both were backed by efficient fielding.

So England's target to win the series was 297, on a pitch which was still showing no signs of undue misbehaviour. Still, Blackham made the sensible observation that he 'would much rather have them than have to make them.' This seemed more so the case when Brockwell failed again that evening. Having hit dreamy-eyed Harry Trott's first delivery of the innings for a heartening four, he top-edged an attempted pull at Giffen, who held the catch at the second attempt. In came Stoddart, to survive the session with Ward, though only just, for a snick went close to Giffen; somebody mused that a young 'gymnast' like Albert Trott might have thrown himself across and held the catch. Bruce stood extremely close at silly mid-on to Ward, but the batsman coolly held on, with England 28 for 1 at the close, 269 from victory. It was a very long road, but all Melbourne, all Australia, all the Empire was agog.

FIFTH DAY

Sorrow was felt for England when the Wednesday dawned wet. This time the pitch would be rendered next to impossible for *them*, as it had for Australia at Sydney in the first Test. But the sympathy, such as it was, was premature, for the rain was shortlived and actually served to bind the cracks in the pitch. The light remained soft, ideal for batting, in contrast to the usual blinding glare which had troubled several of the visiting players.

At a court hearing in Melbourne that morning, a man was had up on an assault charge from the evening before, following a 'discussion' on the relative merits of Australian and English cricketers. 'I meant no harm, Your Honour,' pleaded the defendant. 'Give me another innings and it won't happen again.' The judge gave him six months, and then joined the rush to the MCG for the big match. It was to be the day of a greater judgment.

The big attendance on the final day took the match aggregate beyond 100,000 for the first time in Australia (or perhaps anywhere), and the takings of £4004 were a record too. And the drama flared instantly. Harry Trott's first ball passed Stoddart's bat as he played to leg and the appeal prompted Jim Phillips' finger to be raised. England 28 for 2, the captain gone, and around the chattering ground the feeling spread that this would be Australia's day.

'Stoddy' trailed slowly off, his left hand to his face all the way to the pavilion gate, latecomers wondering what the roar had signified, and word spreading across the park and into the city.

In strode JT Brown, a sturdy little figure, jaw prominent. Someone was piping out *Rule Britannia* on a tin whistle across in the outer, which might have inspired him, for he launched into Trott's first ball, and edged it close to Giffen. Again, a 'gymnast' might have aborted this innings at the moment of its beginning. But Brown scuttled two, and slammed a cut to the boundary before making the best of Giffen's varying length, the strong wind making it difficult for bowlers as they settled to their task. With the uncertainty about the weather, it seemed to be England's policy to go for the runs in case it rained later, with glue-making hot sun possibly to follow. Brown made no secret of his intentions.

He was neither hesitant nor elegant. He just belted the ball through the off side and pulled it with all his might to the leg fence, and with Ward as almost dumb partner, Brown was 26 after 12 minutes in the middle, 35 after 18, with his half-century coming in the record time of 28 minutes. Most of his shots sped across the grass, but a few were airborne, two just over Bruce's head close to the wicket, another high over cover point. Albert Trott's superb stop at cover saved an even faster fifty for Brown, whose skill impressed everyone, including a woman who was overheard saying, 'The Australians never field where Brown hits them!'

While Ward showed the greatest caution (five runs while his partner was scoring 51), Brown hit Giffen seemingly at will, until the maestro decided prudently to remove himself from the attack and give Albert Trott a bowl. If only he could repeat his eight-wicket performance from Adelaide.

McKibbin was tried too, but England's Northerners resisted the lot, darting quickly between wickets when Brown was not hitting fours, the sky beginning to darken. The musician changed his tune to *Daisy Bell* and then *Sweet Marie*.

Gregory surprised with a misfield, and it came home to many watchers that England's field-placing over previous days had to be regarded as strategically better than Australia's now seemed, though when somebody such as Jack Brown was on the rampage, miscuing when he wasn't hitting powerfully and true, then any captain's layout could be made to look naive.

The hundred came, and such was the charm of Albert Ward's cutting that the assembly clapped as if he were one of their own. Giffen consulted with Bruce, Jarvis and the Trott brothers, and

Jack Brown, the sturdy Yorkshireman, whose recordbreaking 140 proved to be his innings of a lifetime.

"OVER!"

Mr. St-dd-rt, Captain of the English Eleven, with Mr. G-ff-n, the Australian Captain, sing in harmony—

| "THE LION AND THE KANGAROO | THE LION LICKED THE KANGAROO— |
| FIGHTING FOR THE CROWN, | HELPED BY MR. BROWN!" |

, *"Mr. BROWN was 'caught' with 140 to his credit."—Times' Report.*

Top: Laurels to Stoddy while Giffen ruefully looks on.

Bottom: It's all over: the fifth Test, at Melbourne, is won and lost, and as the players leave the field for the farewell drinks and handshakes, frayed nerves are left to recover.

inevitably brought himself back on, but it made no difference. By lunch, after 80 minutes' play, Brown and Ward had added 117, Brown on 80, Ward 41; 152 still needed.

Ward, on 54, might have edged a ball to Jarvis, but Phillips was unsighted and rejected the appeal, and when Brown, on 84, nicked a fast one through the slips, Giffen, possibly standing too close, could only get his fingers to it. Lunchtime hopes that Albert Trott might prosper from the Richmond end were evaporating.

Brown's crowning moment came with a big four off Harry Trott's legspin followed by an all-run four in the direction of the Press-box, and a square-leg hit off the same bowler to raise his century. It had come in 95 minutes, bettered only by Jessop (75 minutes) for England and Darling (91) and Trumper (94) for Australia in the 100 years which followed. And his skipper, who was sitting with Lady Hopetoun, 'cool as a cucumber, applauding both sides impartially', could barely conceal his delight.

Another reminder of Ward's presence came with a straight-drive into the crowd for a 'fiver' off Giffen, but to suggestions later that he had, not for the first time, kept himself on rather too long, Giffen claimed that Harry Trott had told him: 'Better stay on.'

Jarvis now put Brown down on 125, and soon the 200 partnership was posted, to be followed by a new Test record stand for any wicket as the 207 by Billy Murdoch and 'Tup' Scott (The Oval, 1884) was passed.

The stand was worth 210 (in only 145 minutes), and had taken England to the brink of victory, when Brown was out, steering McKibbin to slip, where Giffen was able to spare his puffed right hand by holding a left-handed catch. His 140, at practically a run a minute, included 16 fours, and closed to the sound of generous clapping not only from the vast audience but from the Australian players too. It was an inspired knock, his only Test century, and the greatest performance of his life, notwithstanding the two triple-centuries for Yorkshire which were still to come.

Now, with 59 needed and seven wickets in hand, MacLaren joined Ward, whose century was in sight. But at 93 he was yorked by Harry Trott after a beautifully-crafted 3½-hour innings, and it was said that even his opponents felt slightly sad at his missing a hundred. Apart from the big hit off Giffen, Ward had found the fence only six times; but he knew his task was to support Brown as the rugged Yorkshireman played his truly phenomenal innings.

Peel had taken the winning wicket for England in the first Test, at Sydney, and in the second, at Melbourne, and now he secured a distinguished hat-trick by hitting the winning runs in the fifth Test, whacking a Harry Trott full-toss through the off side. England by six wickets, wrapping up the first great Test series.

As the cheering receded, Giffen shook Stoddart's hand and said, in choked voice, 'It's hard to have to congratulate you, Stoddy, old boy.' He apologised for the hesitancy in his voice, but it seems he had already composed a victory speech for himself. He would have cheered up some time later when he was presented with 400 sovereigns from the public for his services to Australian cricket.

Peel gave his bat to Charlie Turner, but the greatest trophy, the ball, had been retrieved at the end by McKibbin. Stoddart had said to Blackham, 'Do you think there is a possible chance of getting that ball? I'd give my very soul to get it, upon my word I would.' So the grizzled Australian wicketkeeper probed the possibilities.

'The ball's very valuable to me,' retorted McKibbin, the young Test debutant. 'I prize it greatly.' Or perhaps he was teasing. Anyway, the plaintive look in 'Stoddy's' eyes persuaded him: 'If you give me your photo,' bargained McKibbin, 'I'll give you the ball.' The dressing-room transaction complete, the England captain expressed his pleasure at the 'nice way in which McKibbin met him'. What became of that historic ball nobody now seems to know. The Bulletin did record, however, that Stoddart held it aloft and said, 'I'm glad Turner hadn't the handling of it.'

In the pavilion was Lord Hopetoun, popular Governor of Victoria and soon to become Australia's first Governor-General upon the inauguration of the Commonwealth on January 1, 1901, when Federation became a reality, Australia's cricketers having helped inspire the dream. His Lordship presented bats to Darling and Brown for top-scoring for their respective teams then made a short speech, saying that some of the pleasantest hours of his life had been spent at the Melbourne Cricket Ground. Frank Grey Smith thanked everybody on behalf of Melbourne CC, and complimented Stoddart not only on his victory but on his 'consummate tact and sportsmanlike conduct'. Stoddart made a typically modest, serene and yet heartfelt reply, but poor Giffen was still struggling with his emotions, and managed some generous remarks either side of his expressed disappointment. Although his players were not Englishmen, 'they were sprouts of a magnificent old trunk'.

Meanwhile, in the city streets, so long-faced were passers-by that it was supposed by one observer that 'a stranger would have thought that half the population had died suddenly and the other half was mourning its loss'.

More pragmatically, the *Argus* deduced that 'the whole story is told in this little record as to the fall of the wickets: Two for 28; three for 238. The one satisfactory point to Australians is that they will be able to say long years hence that they were at the match and saw that partnership'.

'Felix' put it another way: 'When Stoddart fell leg-before first ball, I doubt whether two batsmen ever faced the music with a heavier responsibility upon them than Albert Ward and Jack Brown. And so long as cricket flourishes their splendid performance deserves to hold a high place in the annals of the game as one of the greatest, if not the greatest, performance on record.'

From a vantage-point way in the future, it seems that AE Stoddart was born expressly to govern this fabulous series of Test matches. Nothing in his heroic sporting life before or afterwards touched this sublime peak.

No periodical captured the glory of the moment better than *Melbourne Punch*, one of whose versifiers came up with:

There went a tale to England,
'Twas of the Test match won,
And nobly had her cricketers
That day their duty done.
They didn't fail like funkers,
They kept up England's tail,

They kept their pros from off the booze
And knew they could not fail.

Then wrote the Queen of England,
Whose hand is blessed by God,
'I must do something handsome
For my dear victorious Stod.
Let him return without delay,
And we will dub him pat—
A baronet that he may be
Sir Andrew Stoddart, Bat (Baronet).'

Despite the cartoonists' hints, no national honours ever did come Stoddart's way.

FIFTH TEST MATCH

Melbourne Cricket Ground, March 1, 2, 4, 5, 6, 1895
Toss: Australia
Debuts: Australia–TR McKibbin
12th Men: CTB Turner (Aust). No 12th named for Eng
Umpires: T Flynn and J Phillips
Attendances: 18,000, 29,123, 19,200, 13,500, 14,259. Total: 103,636 Receipts: £4004
Close of play: 1st day Aust 4-282 (Gregory 70, Darling 72); 2nd day Eng 4-200
(MacLaren 40, Peel 18); 3rd day Aust (2) 1-69 (GHS Trott 37, Giffen 14); 4th day
Eng (2) 1-28 (Ward 6, Stoddart 11).

AUSTRALIA
First Innings / Second Innings

Batsman	First Innings		Second Innings	
GHS Trott	b Briggs	42	b Peel	42
W Bruce	c MacLaren b Peel	22	c & b Peel	11
*G Giffen	b Peel	57	b Richardson	51
FA Iredale	b Richardson	8	b Richardson	18
SE Gregory	c Philipson b Richardson	70	b Richardson	30
J Darling	c Ford b Peel	74	b Peel	50
JJ Lyons	c Philipson b Lockwood	55	b Briggs	15
H Graham	b Richardson	6	lbw b Richardson	10
AE Trott	c Lockwood b Peel	10	b Richardson	0
†AH Jarvis	not out	34	not out	14
TR McKibbin	c Peel b Briggs	23	c Philipson b Richardson	13
Extras	(b3, lb10)	13	(b5, lb6, nb2)	13
Total	(148.4 overs, 390 mins)	414	(123.2 overs, 345 mins)	267

Fall: 40, 101, 126, 142, 284, 286, 304, 335, 367

Fall (2): 32, 75, 125, 148, 179, 200, 219, 219, 248

BOWLING	O	M	R	W	w/nb		O	M	R	W	w/nb
Richardson	42	7	138	3	- -		45.2	7	104	6	- -
Peel	48	13	114	4	- -		46	16	89	3	- -
Lockwood	27	7	72	1	- -		16	7	24	0	- 2
Briggs	23.4	5	46	2	- -		16	3	37	1	- -
Brockwell	6	1	22	0	- -						
Ford	2	0	9	0	- -						

ENGLAND
First Innings / Second Innings

Batsman	First Innings			Second Innings	
A Ward	b McKibbin	32	(2)	b GHS Trott	93
W Brockwell	st Jarvis b GHS Trott	5	(1)	c & b Giffen	5
*AE Stoddart	st Jarvis b GHS Trott	68		lbw b GHS Trott	11
JT Brown	b AE Trott	30		c Giffen b McKibbin	140
AC MacLaren	hit wkt b GHS Trott	120		not out	20
R Peel	c Gregory b Giffen	73		not out	15
WH Lockwood	c GHS Trott b Giffen	5			
FGJ Ford	c AE Trott b Giffen	11			
J Briggs	c GHS Trott b Giffen	0			
†H Philipson	not out	10			
T Richardson	lbw b GHS Trott	11			
Extras	(b8, lb8, w4)	20		(b6, lb5, w2, nb1)	14
Total	(133.0 overs, 350 mins)	385		(88.1 overs, 215 mins) (4 wkts)	298

Fall: 6, 110, 112, 166, 328, 342, 364, 364, 366

Fall (2): 5, 28, 238, 278

BOWLING	O	M	R	W	w/nb		O	M	R	W	w/nb
Giffen	45	13	130	4	- -	(2)	31	4	106	1	- -
GHS Trott	24	5	71	4	- -	(1)	20.1	1	63	2	- 1
AE Trott	30	4	84	1	4 -		19	2	56	0	- -
McKibbin	29	6	73	1	- -		14	2	47	1	2 -
Bruce	5	1	7	0	- -		3	1	10	0	- -
Lyons							1	0	2	0	- -

ENGLAND WON BY 6 WICKETS

TEST AVERAGES

AUSTRALIA
Batting

	M	I	NO	R	HS	Avge	100	50
AE Trott	3	5	3	205	85*	102.50	-	2
G Giffen	5	9	0	475	161	52.78	1	3
H Graham	2	3	0	121	105	40.33	1	-
SE Gregory	5	9	0	362	201	40.22	1	1
JM Blackham	1	2	0	76	74	38.00	-	1
FA Iredale	5	9	0	337	140	37.44	1	2
GHS Trott	5	9	0	264	95	29.33	-	1
J Darling	5	9	0	258	74	28.67	-	3
W Bruce	4	7	0	197	80	28.14	-	2
ST Callaway	1	2	0	52	41	26.00	-	-
AH Jarvis	4	7	2	110	34*	22.00	-	-
JJ Lyons	3	6	0	112	55	18.67	-	1
TR McKibbin	1	2	0	36	23	18.00	-	-
CTB Turner	3	5	2	52	26*	17.33	-	-
CE McLeod	1	2	1	17	15	17.00	-	-
E Jones	1	2	1	12	11*	12.00	-	-
JC Reedman	1	2	0	21	17	10.50	-	-
A Coningham	1	2	0	13	10	6.50	-	-
J Worrall	1	2	0	11	11	5.50	-	-
J Harry	1	2	0	8	6	4.00	-	-
H Trumble	1	2	0	3	2	1.50	-	-
H Moses	1	1	0	1	1	1.00	-	-

AUSTRALIA
Bowling

	O	M	R	W	Avge	Best
ST Callaway	33.3	14	56	5	11.20	5-37
CTB Turner	187.1	76	349	18	19.39	5-32
AE Trott	79	17	192	9	21.33	8-43
JC Reedman	9.3	2	24	1	24.00	1-12
G Giffen	354.2	111	820	34	24.12	6-155
GHS Trott	102.5	17	296	12	24.67	4-71
H Trumble	35.1	10	87	3	29.00	3-15
A Coningham	31	9	76	2	38.00	2-17
W Bruce	12	2	38	1	38.00	1-21
CE McLeod	44	9	92	2	46.00	2-67
E Jones	38	7	101	2	50.50	1-44
TR McKibbin	43	8	120	2	60.00	1-47
FA Iredale	2	1	3	0	-	-
JJ Lyons	7	3	17	0	-	-

AUSTRALIA
Fielding

Catches	6 – G Giffen, FA Iredale, GHS Trott
	5 – W Bruce, J Darling, SE Gregory
	4 – AE Trott
	3 – J Worrall
	2 – E Jones, H Trumble, CTB Turner
	1 – JM Blackham, H Graham, J Harry, AH Jarvis, CE McLeod, JC Reedman
Stumpings	7 – AH Jarvis
	1 – JM Blackham

ENGLAND
Batting

	M	I	NO	R	HS	Avge	100	50
JT Brown	5	10	2	343	140	42.88	1	1
A Ward	5	10	0	419	117	41.90	1	2
AE Stoddart	5	10	1	352	173	39.11	1	1
AC MacLaren	5	10	1	240	120	26.67	1	-
FGJ Ford	5	9	0	168	48	18.67	-	-
R Peel	5	10	1	168	73	18.67	-	2
LH Gay	1	2	0	37	33	18.50	-	-
J Briggs	5	9	0	164	57	18.22	-	1
WH Lockwood	5	7	2	89	33*	17.80	-	-
W Brockwell	5	10	0	171	49	17.10	-	-
H Philipson	4	7	1	62	30	10.33	-	-
T Richardson	5	9	3	58	12*	9.67	-	-

ENGLAND
Bowling

	O	M	R	W	Avge	Best
T Richardson	291.2	63	849	32	26.53	6-104
R Peel	305.1	77	721	27	26.70	6-67
J Briggs	150.3	25	436	15	29.07	4-65
AE Stoddart	3	0	31	1	31.00	1-31
W Brockwell	77	26	238	5	47.60	3-33
WH Lockwood	123.5	31	339	5	67.80	1-17
FGJ Ford	34	6	129	1	129.00	1-47

ENGLAND
Fielding

Catches
8 – H Philipson
6 – R Peel
5 – J T Brown, FGJ Ford
4 – W Brockwell
3 – J Briggs, LH Gay, WH Lockwood
2 – A C MacLaren, AE Stoddart
1 – T Richardson, A Ward

Stumpings
2 – H Philipson
1 – LH Gay

CHAPTER FIFTEEN

Gliding Home

Even had the Queen really commanded Stoddart to return home 'without delay', it would have meant cancelling a further four matches. Today, a Test tour would finish with the final Test match, and everybody would be lifted home almost at the speed of sound in a Boeing 747, rather than with seaborne pleasure over a period of weeks.

Now, the English cricketers, on a wave of euphoria, had what was classified as a holiday trip to Tasmania, though Johnny Briggs might have wished it was a weekend in Blackpool, for he was thrown from his bunk during SS *Coogee's* choppy crossing of Bass Strait.

They played an Eighteen of Northern Tasmania on a turf pitch at Launceston, with only 14 of the locals permitted to field at any one time, and with Richardson and Peel rested from the English XI following their big efforts in the Melbourne Test. Ward and Brown might almost have qualified to the same degree for a rest after their amazing efforts. *The Sportsman* felt that the 'severe mental strain' imposed on them made that stand of 210 'the finest performance ever witnessed on the cricket field'. And yet ... some of those watching might have suffered more.

From Mrs Huston's Launceston Hotel, Jack Brown finally got

down to writing a letter home to his parents, brother and sister. 'As you can imagine,' he scratched with his quill-pen, 'we are all very happy now that we have won the final test match and what a match it was. The greatest match on record. The excitement was intense. We outplayed them at every point. When we had 297 to get to win and Brockwell was out at 6 (5 actually) and then Stoddart at 28 the betting men offered 5 to 1 against us. If I ever felt determined to do well I did when I heard the people say "It's all over now". I got 51 in 27 minuites (sic) and then the people began to think that "It was not all over yet" and it was not for Albert Ward and myself took the score to 238 before I was out. Of course you will have read all about the match before you recieve (sic) this letter but I am glad to say that everybody gave us great credit for winning. It was a glorious win one that we shall never forget. The gate reciepts (sic) were 4003£ so you me (may) guess what a lot of people saw the match. The cricketers out here are very good players indeed and take a lot of beating.'

Brown's description of the voyage to Tasmania was less enthusiastic: 'the ship rolled awfully and nearly everybody was bad'. He remarked on his recurring ill-health, saying that he was 'very bad' at the start of the final Test but recovered for the last two days, which was just as well for England. While having made many friends during the tour, he was now eager to get back to Yorkshire.

The three-day match in Launceston was drawn, Humphreys coming back onto the scene with 10 for 98, and being hit twice clean out of the ground by Russell Westbrook, 'a typical Cornstalk, standing 6ft 4in in height, and extremely slim'. After a Sunday of rest, it was Stoddart's 32nd birthday, and the local ladies did him proud with a cake, iced in team colours. The gossip columns still sprouted theories about the various cricketers' romances, and also as to their livelihoods. 'Stoddart and Philipson,' speculated one paper, 'are the only ones with any money at all, each possessing an income of five or six hundred a year. The former is a stockbroker in London, and the latter does nothing.'

Stoddart marked his birthday with a nice 73 not out, following Brockwell's return to better touch with 69, but Briggs strained a leg

/

LAUNCESTON HOTEL
MRS HUSTON
LAUNCESTON
TASMANIA

Brisbane Street
Launceston March 15th 1895

Dear Father and Mother, Brother and Sister

It gives me pleasure to write you a few lines and let you know how we are going on. As you can imagine we are all very happy now that we have won the final test-match and what a match it was. The greatest match on record. The excitement was intense. We outplayed them at every point. When we had 297 to get to win, and Brockwell was out at 6 and then Stoddart at 28 the betting men offered 5 to 1 against us. If I ever felt determined to do well I did when I heard the people say 'Its all over now.' I got 51 in 24 minutes and then the people

Jack Brown's letter home, describing his historic innings.
'The cricketers out here,' he wrote, 'are very good players
indeed and take a lot of beating.'
Courtesy of David Wells

2

began to think that "It was not all over yet" and it was not for Albert Ward and myself took the score to 23? before I was out. Of course you will have read all about the match before you recieve this letter but I am glad to say that everybody gave us great credit for winning. It was a glorious win one that we shall never forget. The gate reciepts were 4003£ so you me guess what a lot of people saw the match. The cricketers out here are very good players indeed and take a lot of beating. We left Melbourne on Thursday night at 6-30 and arrived here that is Launceston in Tasmania at 2 in the afternoon on Friday after a very rough voyage. It was a terrible night the ship rolled awfully and nearly everybody was bad, but I

3

am glad we came over here for
it is a beautiful colony and some
of the scenery is lovely. This afternoon
Johnny Briggs and myself went
for a drive and we enjoyed it
very much. I am sorry to say that
I do not enjoy good health out
here. When we started the big match
I was very bad but I was allright
the last two days of the match and
it was lucky I was or I could never
have done what I did. I hope you
are all well at home. I think of
you every day and shall be glad
to get back to see you. I have
made a lot of very good friends
out here and I hope I shall come
out again to see them. We are
all busy now buying things to
bring home and I dont know
where they are going to put them

4

on board the ship for amongst us
we have a lot. Well we only have
three weeks more here then we start
for home and I shall be glad for
although I have enjoyed the trip
very much I shall be glad to get
back. I should be glad if when you
recieve this letter you will write at
once and address the letter to
J. S. Brown R. M. S. Ophir, Naples.
Remember me to all the friends any
of you see.
I will conclude now with my Love
to you all from
        Your Affectionate Son
            and Brother
                Jack.
                  7

and dropped out of the match, and when the players were warming up on the final morning, Brown was hit in 'the lower part of the body' and also had to withdraw from the game. The local XVIII batted out for a draw, finishing 219 for 13 wickets after being 113 behind on first innings.

A six-hour night-time rail journey through mountains lit by bushfires took the Englishmen to Hobart, and a wine reception with the mayor was held before play began against Fifteen of Southern Tasmania. Rain marred this visit. Not only was Mount Wellington shrouded in mist, spoiling the sightseeing, but lost playing time affected the finances of the venture, and, almost as bad as this, play was sometimes delayed because some of the English players, mainly the amateurs, were nowhere to be seen. It caused much adverse comment locally.

The first day was washed out; Stoddart then top-scored with 21 in his team's moderate total of 91 (Charles Eady 5 for 60); and the local XV were 189 for 13 (Francis Ford 9 for 56, Sid Howe 51 not out, Eady 35), drawing a soggy match remembered with some bitterness by the Hobart cricket fraternity for the apparent aloofness of the visiting amateurs and for their seeming rudeness in absenting themselves from the official lunch. Two explanations followed: that Jim Phillips, the umpire, had telephoned the ground and ascertained that play would not be possible for some time; and that Stoddart had left a pair of his boots on the hot stove to dry out, remembered this as their carriage was well on its way to the ground, and turned back for fear of having the boots ruined. He actually agreed to play on through some rain—commenting later that batsmen could keep control of the bat only by placing a handkerchief around the handle—saying somebody would catch a cold. It was the captain himself, unfortunately, who caught a heavy one, which developed into a chill.

This caused him to miss the match against Victoria, the team returning in SS *Coogee* to the mainland, Stoddart following direct from Hobart in *Parramatta*.

He was well enough to attend a farewell banquet at the MCG on the second evening of the Victoria match, when flags were draped all around the room, and 150 guests toasted Queen Victoria, the State Governor, and 'Our Guests'. Mr Justice a'Beckett referred back to the thrilling final Test here, when he had watched 'with much the same interest as a father watched his dearly beloved child through a serious illness', and recalled how life in the courtroom was constantly disturbed as pieces of paper bearing the score were handed around. The country might still have to wait some time for federation, but 'the federation of sport was an accomplished fact'.

Melbourne Cricket Club honorary life membership was conferred on each English amateur, and complimentary things were said about the behaviour of the professionals. Such was the acceptance of the times, the discrimination would hardly have been noticed, though one newspaper did express resentment that the 'gentlemen' players sat at the top table while the professionals were 'stowed among the crowd'.

Greeted tumultuously, Andrew Ernest Stoddart stood and was eventually allowed to start his speech of thanks, which was delivered in his usual soft and kindly manner. He said all the right things, and singled out Major Wardill and Mr Sheridan, the representatives of the Melbourne and Sydney organisations, who had escorted the team like fathers and seen to all of its needs. He had greatly enjoyed his previous tours, with Lord Hawke's team in 1887-88 and Lord Sheffield's in 1891-92, but this surpassed them. He spoke well of the umpiring standards, and said how much he looked forward to Australia's next visit to England. The cheering was almost incessant, the diners feeling good after their 'Stoddart Pudding' and imported and Australian wines.

Soon everyone was making speechlets: Johnny Briggs, MacLaren, Ford and Philipson, and some cricket-loving politicians, and there were songs and recitations before a halt was called at half-past-11.

The Stoddartless Stoddart's XI lost the three-day match against Victoria, staged in an effort to boost the Victorian Cricket Association's sagging receipts. Play took place on March 21, 22 and 25, the Saturday (23rd) being kept clear so as not to interfere with the race meeting at Flemington, which was a farewell to the departing Governor, Lord Hopetoun.

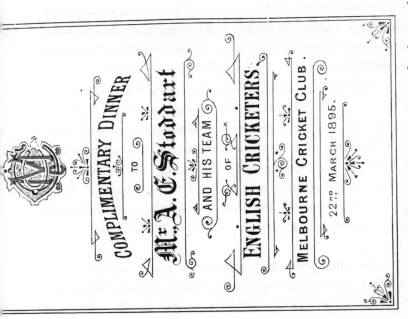

Menu for the farewell banquet, with a photograph taken during the classic Melbourne Test serving as a fond reminder.

The attendance was low—under 3000 paying customers on each of the first two days, only 1000 on the third—because, it was assumed, there had been a surfeit of cricket, and feelings of gloom still hung in the air after Australia's defeat in the decisive Test. Victoria's victory should have had a cheering effect.

Harry Trott put the English XI in and took 8 for 63 in 24.5 overs with brisk legspin, packing the tourists away for 131. Ward and Brown, who had captured the last Melbourne Test with their stand of 210, now made five runs between them. MacLaren top-scored with 43, and Victoria took a big lead by making 269 in the perfect autumn weather (Bruce 42, Albert Trott 46, Charles McLeod 52, new boy Peryman 40), with stand-in English captain Philipson switching his bowling around but suffering mild anguish at the poor fielding.

When the Englishmen batted again, Alf Johns, Victoria's new wicketkeeper, again made a good impression. But for Ford's 85, which included a five off Trumble almost into the elms, England would not have averted an innings defeat. As it was, their 270 left Victoria needing 133, a target they reached with ease, Bruce hitting 72 not out, Albert Trott 44, after Lockwood's dismal tour now saw him flooring a hot catch off Peel's first ball to Bruce at the start.

That evening the touring cricketers were entertained at a dance in Prahran Town Hall, and then came the final leg of the tour which had begun six months earlier. They left Spencer Street station on the Adelaide express, with the departing Lord and Lady Hopetoun as fellow passengers.

Stoddart still did not feel well enough to take the field, so Hylton Philipson again led the side in the 23rd and final match of the tour. And it produced some fairly momentous performances before its conclusion on the fifth evening, good attendances having peaked at 7000 on the Saturday.

Less than a fortnight after his 18th birthday, Clem Hill, a left-hander who was to become one of the greatest of Australian batsmen, went in at No. 8 with South Australia's score 124 for 6 and made 150 not out. He and Walter Giffen (81) put on 192 for the eighth wicket in 2¾ hours, and when the innings closed for

397, young Hill had been in for four hours, not only taking all that Richardson (5 for 148), Peel and the others could direct at him but cutting, pulling and driving them at every opportunity. It was an exquisite bonus for Australian cricket in the last gasps of the 1894-95 season, and it had the band mockingly playing '*E Dunno Where 'E Are* as one of the English fieldsmen–striding like a tired emu–chased laboriously after a drive into the longfield from which five runs were taken.

And then when the Englishmen batted, Hill kept wicket, Affie Jarvis having been extensively injured when thrown from his carriage on the way home after the opening day's play. Hill wore the keeper's gloves for a very long time too. Albert Ward saw out the second day, batted all through the third, and after the Sunday of rest, was out on the fourth day for 219, which was to remain the highest of his 29 first-class centuries. He had stands of 174 with Jack Brown (101) and 181 with FGJ Ford (106). Bobby Peel's 57 helped bulk up the total to 609 in under eight hours, and George Giffen bowled very nearly half the overs to return figures of 87-12-309-5. This was the first instance of any bowler conceding anything near 300 runs in an innings, and Giffen, 36, was just the man to 'achieve' it. Not until Arthur Mailey's famous 4 for 362 in 1926-27 was the record broken.

Hill went in at No. 5 in South Australia's second innings and added a 56 to his unbeaten 150, heading the innings of 255 which left the Englishmen only 44 runs to win–though only 20 minutes' play remained that day. Brockwell and Ford knocked them off in 17 minutes. That evened the score for their defeat in the opening match of the tour.

There remained one further major social occasion, Sir Edwin Smith, the Governor, entertaining both teams and a host of notables at The Acacias, and speech followed speech. Giffen was 'very proud of Master Clem Hill's grand performance', and he expressed regret that 'Stoddy' had been forced to miss this last match. Major Wardill spoke with feeling, and said that when the English cricketers had gone it would leave a big blank in his life, such a splendid time had he had with them on tour. Songs followed, Stoddart having spoken for the last time, saying that in spite of his dislike for speechmaking, he regretted that this was the final effort on his part after such an enjoyable expedition. Again, he said all the right things.

The eight professionals in his troupe presented him with a silver tobacco jar, Johnny Briggs making a pleasant little address, Stoddart almost too choked to respond. The gift had been prompted, said Briggs, by feelings that ran even deeper than respect—feelings of love. Stoddart gave a diamond scarf-pin to each of his players. The tourists had indeed been a harmonious bunch.

And so ended the 1894-95 tour, which had generated such interest in Australia and England that Test cricket was now on a high plane, its 'profile' recognisable for the pattern of play, the intensity of competition, and the massive public interest which still envelops Ashes cricket. Such an elevation of stature might now seem inevitable. It was anything but that. Had the English team not played so attractively and been so genuinely popular, had Australia not fought back in the third and fourth Tests to set up the final cliffhanger, had not the series been projected at such cost, as never before, by the *Pall Mall Gazette* and other publications, the trough into which cricket—even international cricket—had settled might have been sustained and even deepened.

'It has been left to Mr Stoddart and his companions,' stated one editorial, 'to take the Australian public by storm, and for at least four months to make cricket the question of the day. Politics local and Imperial, the war in the East, currency tangles and municipal corruption in the United States, diplomatic intriguing, with possibly grave complications resulting therefrom, have been cast into the shade. Nothing, in short, has been able to withstand the avalanche-like progress of the Stoddart combination.'

CHAPTER SIXTEEN

What Became of Them

RMS *Ophir* returned 10 of the English team home, Ford, Gay and MacLaren leaving Australia separately. And when the ship reached Plymouth, the three Surrey players, Richardson, Brockwell and Lockwood, took the train home, straight into a match against Leicestershire at The Oval. Three Northerners, Peel, Briggs and Ward, also left the ship to hurry home by train, leaving only four, Stoddart, Humphreys, Philipson and Brown, together with Jim Phillips, the Victoria/Middlesex umpire/player, to stay aboard as *Ophir* made up the English Channel to Tilbury.

There, the suntanned skipper stepped ashore into the spring sunshine, a banjo peeping out from his luggage as the jostling crowd let out its cries of welcome. Having talked freely to reporters on the train into London, Stoddart headed off straightaway to his club ground at Hampstead, where a match was in progress against Stoics, victims of his world record 485 nearly nine years earlier.

He was given a grand dinner by the club a few nights later, at the Cafe Monico, attended by *Peter Pan* creator JM Barrie and many other celebrities, the greatest of all WG Grace, who dashed across from Bristol, having just scored his 100th century, 288 against Somerset. It was a glittering evening, leaving 'Stoddy's' hand more numb than ever from all the handshaking. How could he have been happier? Top of the tour averages with 51, his backers delighted with a profit of £7000, a smooth voyage home, and a new season unfolding. His pleasure showed in his speech. And towards the end he was called upon to propose a toast to 'the Press', a duty he performed with greater willingness than many of his successors down the years.

Up in Yorkshire, Jack Brown (who had somehow managed to leave his tour fee of £300 untouched to date) was given a gold watch, solid-silver tea service and a purse of gold after a brass-band reception in Halifax, where crowds lined the streets, while Bobby Peel was given a splash dinner in his hometown, Morley. Peel probably remains the most likely candidate as the subject of a comment in one of the papers in its tour summary: 'The champion grogster' during the tour 'had so many fines for "unfitness to play" entered against his name that he finished up, it is said, with a debit balance.'

But as the 1895 English cricket season engulfed them, they were heroes all, the men who had beaten a full-strength Australia to hold the Ashes on foreign fields.

*　　*　　*　　*　　*

Life, like an innings, is fragile: safe only as far as the next breath, the next ball. Eight of England's 13 on the 1894–95 tour made it to the age of 65 and beyond, the last dying as late as 1949. Of the 22 Australians who played in the series, 11 reached 65, the last fading away in 1946.

JOHNNY BRIGGS died in Cheadle Asylum on January 11, 1902, his last years dogged by mental instability allied to his epileptic condition. He had returned to Australia with Stoddart's second team, in 1897–98, but was one of the many who enjoyed little success, and in 1899, during the Headingley Test, he suffered a violent seizure while at the theatre, and was taken into shelter. He did re-emerge, and took over 100 wickets in 1900, including 10 for 55 for Lancashire against Worcestershire; but this was to be his last season.

Institutionalised again, he went into a world of his own, and was sometimes seen in the corridors, bowling an imaginary ball. With the real ball he had taken 2221 wickets at only 15.95 apiece, and his 118 Test wickets had cost little more. He made over 14,000 runs too, at 18.28, with 10 centuries, one of them in an Australian Test. His death at 39 was deeply mourned by his wife and twin boys, as well as the cricket world at large.

JACK BROWN, a heavy-smoking asthmatic, remained a prodigious rungetter from this tour, when he was 25, until 1903, establishing the finest of opening partnerships with John Tunnicliffe for Yorkshire, crowned by their record first-wicket stand of 554 against Derbyshire at Chesterfield in 1898, which came after a recuperative winter in South Africa. But he played for England only three times after the 1894–95 tour, making a highest score of 36. He suddenly became teetotal, pouring his remaining beer down the kitchen sink; but he could not give up smoking. When he had a heart attack, a friend, who was a valet to King Edward VII, told His Majesty, who sent his own doctor to look at Brown. He had a highly profitable benefit in 1901, but his captain, Lord Hawke, while acknowledging JT Brown's skill and previously admirable qualities, felt that his sensational century at Melbourne made him a little boastful, and that he was too figure-conscious and too keen to monopolise the strike. Leaving a wife, Jennie, and a family, Brown died in a London nursing-home on November 4, 1904, aged 35, from 'congestion of the brain and heart failure'.

HARRY GRAHAM, the dashing 'natural' batsman with the unique double of a century in his first Test innings in both England and Australia, toured England a second time in 1896 but failed to make a century, was troubled by poor health, and managed no better than a duck and 10 at Lord's in his only Test appearance. A few years later he moved to New Zealand, and played for Otago, now bowling legspin in support of his electrifying batting. But when he lost his place in the side, he drifted into melancholia. He had thought about studying dentistry and had coached cricket at a school in Dunedin, but always he seemed to lack the ability to apply himself. A 'hopeless case', he was admitted to an asylum in Dunedin and died there on February 7, 1911, aged 40. As JN Pentelow put it in *Cricket*, 'To the man who has been slowly dying for years, "going at the top first", like the great Dean Swift and Robert Southey, death comes as a happy release. But one cannot help but sorrow when one thinks of "the little dasher", as Tom Horan named him, as he was in 1893, good-looking, bright-faced, clean-limbed, grand bat, and splendid field, seeming then embarked on a fair course, with flags flying and all sails set, and then reflect on the shipwreck that he, or circumstances too strong for him, made of his life.'

TOM RICHARDSON, Titan among fast bowlers, showed no ill-effects after his strenuous Australian tour, taking an astonishing 290 wickets at 14.37 in the 1895 English season which followed. He remained the world's premier fast bowler for several summers to come, and toured Australia again with Stoddart's side in 1897–98. Now, though, he was that much older, and his exertions began to tell. He also put on too much weight, and his Surrey career ended abruptly, though he took 119 wickets at 22.95 in 1903, his last full season. He went to the West Country and ran a pub. Loved for his great heart and the simplicity and honesty of his approach to cricket and life, on July 2, 1912, he suffered a cerebral haemorrhage and fell to his death while walking near St Jean d'Arvey on a holiday in France. He was 41.

ALBERT TROTT was also only 41 at the time of his death. Following the great disappointment of being omitted from the 1896 Australian tour of England, when his brother was skipper, 'Albatrott' qualified for Middlesex, and from 1898 to 1907 he belted runs and gathered wickets with his unique repertoire at such a rate that it is doubtful if any county ever made a better overseas signing, particularly as his popularity was sky-high, not least because he loved to join the crowd in a drink at the fall of a wicket. At the time, his figures defied belief when he passed 1000 runs and 200 wickets in 1899 and 1900, sealing his immortality with one enormous hit in 1899 which sent the ball over the Lord's pavilion. It was all the sweeter to him in that the Australian, MA Noble, was the bowler. Trott actually played for England, during the 1898-99 tour of South Africa, taking 17 wickets in the two Tests but seeing his astronomical batting average of 102.50 from the 1894-95 series come crashing down to reality. If he is remembered for one other match it was his own benefit match, in 1907, when he took four wickets in four balls and then another hat-trick in Somerset's second innings. He became an umpire, living alone in Willesden and continuing to drink far too much. His dropsy became almost impossible to endure, especially when coupled with his great memories, now fading fast. He shot himself on July 30, 1914, five days before the outbreak of the First World War. He left his wardrobe to his landlady, some photographs to a friend in Australia, and the rest of his 'estate' amounted to £4. MCC met the cost of burial, but it was 79 years before a memorial was placed on the grave, courtesy of Middlesex CCC. A great cricketer somehow wasted: was his county wicket-keeper MacGregor trying to be kind when he told him: 'What a pity you haven't got a head instead of a turnip. You'd be the best bowler in the world'?

AE STODDART committed suicide eight months after Albert Trott. That such a beautiful batsman and universally popular man should be dragged down to that condition makes him one of cricket's outstandingly tragic figures. He had returned to Australia for his fourth tour in 1897-98, but the results were hard for England to swallow. MacLaren led in three of the five Tests, 'Stoddy' being ill and disconsolate following the death of his mother. Australia won the last four Tests, and when he played he batted in the lower order. And there was bitterness at the end when he gave an interview in which he condemned the vicious barracking. Many cricketers and decent spectators knew his words were justified, but his words of mild protest tarnished his image in a country where he had been as highly regarded as any of Australia's own. His appetite for the game was receding, and 1898 was his last full season with Middlesex, though he did come back for JT Hearne's benefit match at Lord's and stroked 221, his highest first-class score, to show that class, even at 37, will seldom be denied. In 1906 he married at last. Ethel

Luckham, a vivacious Australian girl who had met him on his first Australian tour, 18 years previously, became his bride, but could not keep his spirits high enough when illness brought him down and personal isolation and financial anxiety as war raged destroyed his psyche. On Easter Saturday, April 3, 1915, at his home in 115 Clifton Hill, a short walk from the Lord's ground he had graced so often, 'Stoddy' shot himself through the temple. Already, after a 10-year span, his effigy at Madame Tussaud's waxworks exhibition had been put into storage, and, partly because of the stigma attached to his death, his name sank towards obscurity, until a full-length biography of 'my dear victorious Stod' appeared over half-a-century later.

HARRY TROTT, too, did not have an easy middle age. Mental instability saw him in and out of Kew and other asylums several times. He too was genuinely liked by all his team-mates and all his opponents, and when he became captain of Australia on the 1896 tour of England he displayed great tactical acumen. His 143 in the Lord's Test, against an attack which included Richardson, Lohmann and Hearne, was an exceptional innings, and his stand with Gregory of 221 (in under three hours) was a new Test record. Calm and always keen to offer encouragement, Harry Trott, in *Wisden's* subtle words, by sheer force of character 'overcame the disadvantages involved in lack of education'. His four victories over Stoddart's team in the 1897–98 series gave him one of the proudest campaign badges in Australian cricket history. He died on November 10, 1917, aged 51.

CHARLIE MCLEOD had more of an impact when England next toured, in 1897–98, opening the innings and making 112 in the second Test, at Melbourne, and taking 5 for 65 in the next Test, at Adelaide. Always the adjective most readily found for him was 'steady', and he proved that again on the 1899 tour of England, though having to wait until the final Test before breaking back into the team. He then scored 31 not out and 77 to help ensure the draw which tied up the series. Missing the 1902 tour, he went to England again in 1905, bowing out quietly. His brother, Bob, a year older, had played for Australia before him, and four other brothers played for Melbourne CC and another, Dan, for Victoria. Charlie died in Toorak on November 26, aged 49.

JACK HARRY, although multi-talented, had to make do with his one Test appearance. At least Australia won that one at Adelaide, arresting England's surge in the series. Richardson twice dispatched him cheaply. He came close to further honours when chosen for the 1896 tour of England, but a knee injury caused his invitation to be cancelled, and he saw out his days with Victoria. In the year of his death he had been awarded a benefit match in Bendigo which returned him £200. At the age of 38 he had tried his luck in England, on the MCC groundstaff, but he was not destined to rock county cricket as his fellow Victorian Albert Trott did. Harry died in Canterbury, Victoria on October 27, 1919, aged 62.

SYD CALLAWAY also never played for Australia again after the Adelaide Test of January 1895, despite his 5 for 37 and runs from the No. 11 berth. Having toured New Zealand with NSW sides, he emigrated, played for Canterbury, and for New Zealand representative teams against visiting English and Australian sides. It may safely be assumed that Archie MacLaren was in one of his liverish moods when he declaimed that 'Callaway can't bowl a bit!' He bowled 'Archie Mac' at Adelaide. Callaway, after two years of illness, died in Christchurch, NZ on November 25, 1923, aged 55.

WALTER HUMPHREYS, the grey-haired old buffer who had bemused so many country batsmen on his Australian tour, never did get a Test call-up. He plied his underhand cunning for another couple of seasons, became an umpire for the 1896 summer, and helped Hampshire out in two matches in 1900, when he was 50. His son, also a lob bowler, played a few matches for his father's county, Sussex, between 1898 and 1900. Walter senior died in Brighton on March 23, 1924, aged 74.

'DINNY' REEDMAN died two days later, in Adelaide, at the age of 55. He was another who played in only one Test, but it could hardly have been a more memorable game, Australia making 586, bowling England out for 325 and making them follow on, and then losing. Reedman's allround cricket, not least his wonderful fielding, continued to serve South Australia proud for years, his last appearance being in 1908–09. He could never have been more than an aspiring understudy for Giffen, but there was honour in that.

BILLY BRUCE played no more Tests after the 1894–95 series, but was left with a respectable batting average of just on 30 from his 14 Tests, which was higher than his average for Victoria, for whom he played his last match in 1903–04, when he was in his 40th year. At the age of 61, he had begun to drink fairly heavily and his legal practice had known better days. The slim youngster had become a plump man. On August 3, 1925 he kissed his wife goodbye, walked from his home in St Kilda and drowned himself in the sea off Point Ormond.

FRANK IREDALE continued to serve Australia through two tours of England (scoring 108 in the Old Trafford Test of 1896) and in the crushing victories of 1897–98, and played for NSW until the 1901–02 season, finishing with the respectable first-class average of 33.63, with a highest score of 196 against Tasmania. He wrote on the game, and produced a book, *Thirty-Three Years of Cricket*, in 1920, two years before becoming NSWCA secretary. In 1922 he had become a rare beneficiary of an Australian testimonial cricket match, the event returning him the hefty present of £1740. This fine, patient batsman, so often a poor starter, and peerless outfielder, later to become slip catcher for Ernie Jones's thunderbolts, died in North Sydney on April 15, 1926, aged 58.

JACK LYONS played in only one further Test, the first of the 1897–98 series, but his reputation as a violent hitter of the ball was to last some years before the natural process of obscurity took care of it. Some of his explosive innings were standard reference points whenever the subject came up. He batted on for South Australia almost into the 20th Century, pounding eight centuries in all and averaging 34.65, a good figure even allowing for the short side boundaries at Adelaide Oval. In 1925–26, Lyons, a stockbroker, received a benefit, part of the proceeds from South Australia's match against NSW. He died on July 21, 1927, aged 64.

GEORGE GIFFEN, if not among the greatest Australian captains, was decidedly an allrounder of immense value, his stamina being as awesome as his skills and his determination. He was addicted to cricket, playing for South Australia until his 45th year, and taking 15 for 185 and scoring 81 and 97 not out against Victoria when in his 44th year. In all, he scored 11,758 runs at 29.54 in 251 first-class matches, with 18 centuries, and took 1023 wickets at 21.29, 95 times taking five or more wickets in an innings. No cricketer could have found retirement such a repugnant experience, but he retained his interest, coached boys freely, and was gratified to find £2020 raised for him by a testimonial match at Adelaide Oval in 1922–23, when he was just on 64. Joe Darling was the instigator, and Giffen wrote him a warm letter of thanks. 'Your timely and energetic appeal on my behalf,' he wrote, 'has resulted in the rest of my life being at least comfortable.' There was little enough of it left. Giffen died in Parkside, Adelaide on November 29, 1927, aged 68, four months after the passing of that other South Australian cricket giant, JJ Lyons. His mighty contribution to the 1894–95 Test series was rewarded with a presentation of £400, and the Giffen Stand at the Adelaide Oval is a lasting memorial.

SYD GREGORY, who went on playing for his country further into the 20th Century than any of the other combatants in the 1894–95 Test series, became captain of Australia, really by default, during the Triangular Test series in England in 1912, when he was 42. If he was no great leader and tactician, his dapper batsmanship and rapacious fielding kept him in the forefront of Australian cricket well beyond an age when contemporaries had hung up their boots. His long service was saluted with a silver cup and a purse containing £200 in the Lord's Test of 1912 to mark his awesome feat of 50 Test appearances. Modern players can clock up that many Tests in a third of the time. Gregory had already received £630 from a benefit match at Sydney (literally his native ground) in 1906–07. So his long devotion did pay off in the end. He made four Test centuries in all against England, the others coming at Lord's in 1896 (when he and Harry Trott put on 221), The Oval (1899) and

Adelaide (1903–04). A shining star of a cricketer in Australia's formative years, he made 15,190 first-class runs at 28.55, with 25 centuries. Leaving his shop business in the hands of partners, he suffered financial ruin in 1903. It was two years before he was discharged from bankruptcy. Having firstly worked in the Post Office, he later joined the Water Board. His tour fees and profits were more vital than ever. Syd Gregory, an Australian record 58 Tests to his name for years to come, died at home not far from the Sydney Cricket Ground on August 1, 1929, aged 59.

BILL LOCKWOOD eventually put the disappointments of the 1894– 95 tour behind him, accidental injuries and all, and became, by the end of the decade, one of the finest players around. The 1898 season marked his second coming. He had got himself fit, and now his allround play came into its own. Came 1902, and he played a key role in several of the Tests of that exciting series, taking 11 for 76 in the Old Trafford thriller, won by Australia by three runs, having just scored 100 and taken nine wickets for the Players against a glittering Gentlemen side at Lord's. Since he never returned to Australia, those who had watched him on the Stoddart tour must have wondered how Ranjitsinhji could regard Lockwood as the most difficult fast bowler he ever faced. The slump in his career can be attributed to the death of his wife and one of their children. Four times subsequently did he take nine wickets in an innings. He coached after retirement, and played a bit here and there. Then arthritis gripped him, and towards the end he was wheelchair-bound, sometimes sighted at Trent Bridge, back near his birthplace. He rejoiced in the discovery of Harold Larwood in the mid-1920s, and said he was as fast as anything in Victorian times—apart from his old comrade Tom Richardson. Lockwood died in Radford on April 26, 1932, aged 64.

JACK BLACKHAM, 'Prince of Stumpers', had played his last first-class match, and was also the last of the players in the first Test match of all, 18 years earlier, to play Test cricket, another link broken. Now, at last, he could give his nerves a rest, though living off investments was sometimes precarious. Eventually income dropped below expenditure, and this lifelong bachelor fell on hard times. In 1911 the VCA raised £1359 for him through a testimonial, and he lived on into his 79th year, watching matches at the MCG from a high point of the pavilion and passing opinions on the wicketkeepers in action below, usually sympathetically. He was able to see Tests up in Sydney (the setting for his dramatic final appearance in December 1894), thanks to the generosity of friends. Two days before the second Test of the Bodyline series, at the MCG, 'Old Jack' died, on December 28, 1932, aged 78.

'AFFIE' JARVIS, who was in Blackham's shadow for so long, had also played his final Test with the conclusion of the 1894–95 series, though he served South Australia until just into the next century. Jim Kelly took over the keeper's position for Australia. Jarvis, though, performed well for his State, having to take the express bowling of Ernie Jones in addition to Giffen's spin. Had an accident befallen the tough-as-iron Kelly, Australia would have been glad of Jarvis's return. He had the pleasure of seeing his son play in a couple of matches for South Australia in 1905–06. 'Affie' Jarvis, coachbuilder by trade, died on November 15, 1933, aged 73.

BILLY BROCKWELL played in only one further Test for England, at Old Trafford in 1899. But he continued to be of great value to Surrey, following a moderate 1895 after his return from Australia, which nonetheless embraced his lifetime-best bowling figures, 8 for 22 against Warwickshire. Twelfth man for England at The Oval in 1896, he held a brilliant catch at extra cover to dismiss Harry Trott. And the Brockwell-Abel opening partnership for Surrey was probably the best in the land as the last summers of the 19th Century played themselves out. In 1897, 'Brocky' made his highest score, 225 against Hampshire, at The Oval, his first-wicket stand with the odd little Bobby Abel amounting to 379, then a world record. Tall and enduringly handsome, Brockwell usually made his runs fast—and spent some of his evenings dressed like a duke and off to the theatre. Having coached in South Africa, he now took up winter engagements in India, financed by the Maharajah of Patiala, and in 1900 he had a benefit which returned him £490. The runs and wickets suddenly began to slow down, and Tom Hayward took his place as Abel's opening partner. Brockwell's final first-class match was in 1903, malaria contributing to his eclipse. Over the next 30-odd years he went slowly downhill. He once owned some cottages by Ham Common, near Richmond Park, but in time they had to be disposed of. He never married, and was inconsolable when his old team-mate Tom Richardson died in 1912. Coaching, umpiring and occasional journalism enabled him to eke out a living, but it was a poor one. He was seen walking across the Common in a dressing-gown sometimes, and gathering firewood in the park. Managing to desist from seeking charity from Surrey CCC or other sources, Brockwell lived on until the summer of 1935, when, at the age of 70, he was found in a bad way in a barn at the back of the New Inn, and died in an institution on June 30. He was buried nearby in Richmond Cemetery, only a few yards from Richardson.

'PUNCH' PHILIPSON played hardly any further first-class cricket, and spent most of the rest of his life on his estate in Aberdeenshire, Scotland, entertaining friends to weekend shooting parties and suchlike. Shortly after the 1894-95 tour, which Philipson greatly enjoyed, it was said that Stoddart was warmly disposed towards his sister; but nothing came of it. 'Stoddy's' close friend, who outlived him by 20 years, died in London on December 4, 1935, after several years of ill-health. He was 69.

JACK WORRALL came good only once in a while, and this was reflected in the selectors' wavering interest. His two tours of England were 11 years apart—1888 and 1899—and his 11 Test appearances were spread over 14 years, with a highest score of 76 (out of 95 while he was in) at Headingley in 1899, when Noble and Gregory made 'pairs'. In 1896 he had hit 417 not out in a Melbourne district match, his side, Carlton, totalling 922. For Victoria, he scored over 2400 runs and took 74 wickets in an 18-year career which ended abruptly when it was revealed that he had written to an English umpire at the start of Australia's 1902 tour advising him to no-ball Saunders and Noble for throwing. Worrall wrote as 'JW' for *The Australian*, and to him is attributed the coining of the term

'Bodyline' during the acrimonious 1932–33 Ashes series. He died in Fairfield Park, Melbourne on November 17, 1937, aged 76.

HUGH TRUMBLE, who played such an insignificant role in the 1894–95 series, went on to become the leading wicket-taker in Anglo-Australian Tests, his tally of 141 in 31 Tests remaining supreme until Lillee and Botham overtook it. He seemed to improve with each of his five tours of England, the last being made in 1902, and having done the hat-trick against the Old Enemy at Melbourne in 1901–02, he did another to add a sting to his final Test two years later, at the same ground. He took 929 first-class wickets at 18.44, with best figures of 9 for 39 for the 1902 Australians against South of England at Bournemouth. Had there been Man of the Match awards in his time, he would have taken many as his clever and relentless bowling swayed Tests Australia's way. As it was, Trumble, by his great height, was always the most conspicuous of the Australians. For a time he was probably the world's best bowler, and he twice captained Australia, winning the last two Tests in 1901–02. He had met his future bride on the ship going to England in 1899, and in time they had eight children. He gave up his bank job in 1911 and became secretary of Melbourne Cricket Club. In his large grey hat he was the most conspicuous figure on the ground and in the streets of Melbourne, and none was more companionable. He held office for 27 years, dying on August 14, 1938, aged 71.

HARRY MOSES was limited to six Tests, the last being at Sydney in 1895, when Australia drew level at 2-2. Nor did he play for NSW after that season, leaving an exceptional record of 2593 runs for the State at 41.16. Giffen, close to envy at Moses' patient approach, wrote that his leg-glance was outstanding, and, as at 1898, he could still lay claim to having been Australia's second-best batsman; only his never having been tested by English conditions prevented him from standing level with Murdoch. It might have been just as well for England that Richardson bowled him for only 1 in that final appearance at Sydney. Moses, who became chairman of trustees of the SCG, and was a wine merchant, died in Strathfield, Sydney on December 7, 1938, aged 80.

ALBERT WARD, the upright, composed batsman to whom England owed so very much during the 1894-95 series, played no more Tests, despite having his best-ever season upon his return from Australia. Unluckily for him, no country toured England in 1895. He remained one of the most prolific scorers in county cricket, reaching the then-rare seasonal aggregate of 1000 nine times, and carrying his bat through an innings on five occasions. His 219 against South Australia remained the highest of his 29 centuries by his retirement after the 1904 season, and in later life, memories of his success in Australia, when he made most runs (916 to Stoddart's 870) on the tour, warmed him. He died near Bolton on January 6, 1939, aged 73.

ARTHUR CONINGHAM became another one-Test wonder, but at least it permitted a keen monumental mason to inscribe 'International Cricketer' on 'Conny's' gravestone. He played a few more matches for Queensland and NSW, the last in 1898–99, and just when his name seemed to have slipped quietly into the annals, he became the most talked-about man in Sydney when he brought a charge of adultery against a leading Roman Catholic priest, Mrs Coningham being the alleged 'victim'. The case aroused fearful sectarian passions, and was more than usually interesting in that fair-haired, blue-eyed Coningham, swaggering with confidence though ignorant of court procedure, conducted his own case when his counsel walked out. The jury could not agree. Conspiracy was all around as a second trial began, and this time Coningham, who announced that he had received 47 threats by mail, wore a loaded revolver on his belt. It was confiscated. He lost the case. The priest returned to St Mary's in triumph. Coningham sobbed loudly, but later told a rally of Protestants: 'I was friendless and penniless. For four days I fought the Church of Rome with a halfpenny!' He and his wife went to New Zealand, where Coningham was later jailed for fraud. She divorced him in 1912 for alleged adultery in a beach-shed, admitting she had pointed a gun at him but denying breaking a bottle on his head. He in turn said he could not fathom the Law: 'In Sydney, my wife said she did and a jury said she didn't. In Wellington, I said I didn't and a jury said I did.' This was the man who got MacLaren out with his first ball in Test cricket. He died in Gladesville, Sydney on June 13, 1939, aged 75.

Tom McKibbin earned selection for the 1896 tour of England and headed the bowling with 101 wickets at 14.26, playing in two of the three Tests, taking six wickets to help Australia to victory at Old Trafford and five more at The Oval, where his innings of 16 from the No. 11 position dragged Australia up to 44, to lose by 66 runs. All through the tour, however, there were murmurs about his action and natural resentment among opposing sides and onlookers who were convinced that he threw. He played in two Tests in the 1897–98 series before losing his place, the strength of Australian bowling then being quite formidable. His last first-class season was 1898–99, and he went out in style, taking 10 wickets in NSW's match against Tasmania and 7 for 30 in the second innings of a New Zealand XI, also at the SCG, whipping the ball back from outside off stump. His weight increased, though he was still in his twenties, and after missing out on the 1899 tour of England, he spent some time in Western Australia before returning to Bathurst. He became a bit of a swagman, moving from place to place and repairing shearing-machines, but in 1934 he took off to England to see some of the Test matches played by Woodfull's Australians, armed with a letter of introduction from the NSWCA. It had been a meteoric career. McKibbin had gone from Country Week cricket into a Test match in his introductory season, and was finished as a Test bowler at 27. He died at a homestead near Bathurst on December 15, 1939, aged 69.

Francis Ford continued to delight spectators at Middlesex matches for a further five seasons before ill-health persuaded him to retire. The five Tests of 1894–95 were to remain his only England appearances, but his form in 1897, when he topped the national averages, might have earned him another cap had there been a touring team in England other than the Philadelphians. That summer he made 805 runs at 53.67, hitting with great ferocity, fast bowling or slow. He was greatly feared by bowlers in his many club matches. He contributed much to the lbw debate in the 1930s which led to a major amendment. He had never been one to use his pads while he had a bat in his hand. FGJ Ford died in Burwash, Sussex on February 7, 1940, aged 73.

BOBBY PEEL, who administered the *coup de grace* in all three England victories in the 1894–95 Tests, had a longer life than any of the other participants in that epic series, though his career as a Yorkshire cricketer extended no further than 1897. Drink was the almost inevitable cause. He may have been 40, but he was still a valuable bowler. But even George Hirst's protective actions could not save him when he turned up late and hungover (again), tried to prove he was fit by twirling down a ball—except it crashed into the sightscreen—and was sent from the field by his captain Lord Hawke, his cap still askew, his face now permanently reddened. He found employment in the leagues and played on, and though he was not a considerate husband, there were signs of mellowing later in life. He may even have come to regret some of his actions—such as disgracing himself on a shoot with Prince Ranjitsinhji, when Peel blasted eight barrels at a hare, removing its legs, an ear and much else before chasing the remnants of the animal into a neighbouring property, still firing away, until all life was extinguished. The perversity in his character was illustrated by Lord Hawke when he wrote that 'when at his deadliest and congratulated afterwards one could detect no gleam of pleasure on his countenance'. Perhaps the verbal out-take which should signal Peel's spirit best of all was his remark to Stoddart on that day in Sydney in December 1894. Through his alcoholic haze he stared at the wet pitch, and said to his captain, 'Gi' me t'ball, Mr Stoddart. Ah'll get t'boogers out.' Peel died in Morley, near Leeds, on August 12, 1941, aged 84.

ERNIE JONES went on to earn the reputation of Australia's greatest fast bowler, with the possible exception of Gregory or McDonald in the 1920s, until after the Second World War. There was but one reservation. The suspicions about his action climaxed when Jim Phillips no-balled him for throwing both during the South Australia match against Stoddart's 1897–98 team and in the second

Test. Harry Trott guided him through this troubled time, and with a slightly modified action he never again transgressed. His terror bowling claimed stacks of wickets, not least during his three tours of England. On the first, in 1896, he bounced one through WG Grace's beard, earning a rebuke from The Champion. 'Sorry, Doc, she slipped,' was 'Jonah's' immortal reply. In the 1897–98 series he took most wickets (22), sharing with Richardson, who paid 10 runs more per wicket. In 1899, in five Tests, Jones took 26, 11 more than any other bowler in either side, seven of them coming at Lord's—five of them great England batsmen—for 88 as Australia moved to the only decision in the series. Batsmen everywhere were relieved to see his powers finally wane. 'Did you go to Prince Alfred College?' once asked a dignitary. 'Yeah,' said Ernie, 'I used to collect the garbage there.' Later, as a customs officer, he was a familiar sight at the wharf when English teams arrived, yelling a friendly greeting: 'We're gonna tan the hide off ya!' Even at 60 he looked fit and strong enough to do it personally. Jones died in Adelaide on November 23, 1943, aged 74.

CHARLES TURNER had the longest life of all the 1894–95 Australians. The fourth Test, controversially, had been his final Test, with McKibbin, another son of Bathurst, being seen as the new Turner. Having left the Australian Joint Stock Bank, Turner entered business, and after retiring from cricket in 1897 he went to Queensland for a time, living in Gympie. He enjoyed coaching, but only if it meant encouraging natural talent. He sidled up to the young Bill O'Reilly at the nets and congratulated him after hearing him resist Arthur Mailey's suggestion that he should alter his grip. 'Tiger' O'Reilly was to join the elite list of those who have taken 100 wickets in Tests against England, but none has got even close to 'Terror' Turner's average of 16.53. In January 1910 a benefit match was staged for Turner at the SCG, and he played. Now 47, he opened the bowling with Charlie Kelleway, and reduced The Rest to 8 for four wickets, himself bowling Edgar Mayne for 0. It was like old times. He received £331 from the match. In 1926 Turner wrote *The Quest for Bowlers*, a small, rare book which is packed with wisdom. All a student would need, having digested the contents, was Turner's physique and co-ordination, and he too might then take 993 wickets at 14.26. Married for a third time, CTB Turner left £202 when he died on New Year's Day 1944, aged 81. For almost 30 years his ashes remained, unclaimed, in a blue cardboard box in a Sydney funeral parlour. The author was responsible for having them received by Bathurst City Council and interred in the cemetery in Turner's home town.

ARCHIE MACLAREN, as at 1895, had the greatest future of all Stoddart's touring cricketers. Returning to England via Japan, he rocked the cricket world a few weeks later by scoring 424 in 470 minutes for Lancashire against Somerset at Taunton, a new first-class world record. He toured with Stoddart a second time, in 1897–98, and four years later found himself leading the next English team to Australia. By 1909 he had taken his Test appearances to 35, and had made so many runs at Sydney that he was to claim that he only had to poke his tongue out at the ball there and it went for four. Runs rolled from his imperious bat in all parts of the world, even when he was 51, when he made 200 not out against a New Zealand representative XI at Wellington. In 1921 he had been as good as his word by selecting a team, several of them anything but famous, which beat the apparently invincible Australians in a celebrated match at Eastbourne. He had theories, and often he was right, though his England captaincy record was dim: four victories and 11 losses in 22 Tests. Married to a Melbourne girl during the 1897–98 tour, MacLaren earned a living from an assortment of enterprises. Only towards the end did he and Maud feel comfortable, after she had inherited a large sum of money. The dashing batsman who had hammered and charmed 22,236 runs, with 47 centuries, five of them in Tests against Australia, died in Warfield Park, Berkshire on November 17, 1944, aged 72. It was only a month before the 50th anniversary of England's astonishing 10-run win at Sydney.

JOE DARLING had a most distinguished career, on and off the cricket field. He went to England in 1896 and hit a newcomer's record 1555 runs (in 53 innings)—and was also barracked at Lord's in musical fashion, when spectators protested at his dour batting by whistling *Poor Old Joe* and then the *Dead March in Saul*. For perhaps the only time, he displayed irritation. Home again, he became the first batsman to make 500 runs in a Test series when he helped Australia to their 4–1 triumph in 1897–98. He scored three centuries. By 1899 he was the logical choice as Australia's captain, and had the rare distinction of leading his country on three successive England tours, playing in every match and scoring a mighty 1941 runs in 1899, and retaining the Ashes again in 1902, his team that year a frontrunner still for the title Greatest Australian Team. His last tour, in 1905, brought adversity at last, FS Jackson leading England, by personal example, to a 2–0 win. Darling this time piled up 1696 runs, though, like the similarly chunky Allan Border, another left-hander, he now went in at No. 6. Darling led Australia in 21 of his 34 Tests, earning respect for his batsmanship, his tactical sense, and his sheer toughness. His 91-minute century in the last Test of the 1897–98 series, at Sydney, remains a record for Australia against England, shading other sub-100-minute performances by Trumper and Bradman. Had Darling's wealthy father not insisted on setting his son up with a 10,000-acre sheep station in Tasmania, he would have played in several more Tests. But those he did play were among the most famous in history. Retiring at 36, he later entered politics and was elected to the Tasmanian Parliament at 50. He had 12 children. No Australian captain has been more highly regarded, none was tougher, or fairer. Joe Darling died on January 2, 1946, aged 75.

LESLIE GAY was the last of the 1894–95 Test cricketers to die. Keeping wicket for England in the first-up classic at Sydney, where he had such a wretched time of it, he did at least complete four dismissals and contribute a useful 33 to England's first innings. After the tour he played no more first-class cricket until 1900, when he turned out in nine matches for Hampshire, renewing acquaintance with MacLaren and some of the professionals from that Australian tour: Richardson, Lockwood, Brockwell, Brown, Ward. Already that enjoyable expedition of '94–95 under dear old Stoddy was taking on the feel of the good old days. Gay, a tall, proud double international, had been the youngest member of that team. Now he had outlived them all. He died, with the rank of major, in Salcombe, Devon on November 1, 1949. He was 78. He took with him the last authentic first-hand memories of life on that tour, in the hotels and clubs, on board ship, in the dressing-room, out in the heat of the middle, in the First Great Test Series.